"An essential practical read for anyone looking to super-charge their motivation, but more than that it helps you truly understand what you want and why, enabling you to break through and create that vital change. This book undoubtedly will light a fire inside you to create your own unique legacy."
**Ben Griffiths, Creator, The Primal Nation Fitness Revolution & "The UK's go-to-guy for Women's Weight-Loss"**

"*How to Change Your Life* is a book you can pick up at any point and gleam some gems for your day or week. Some of the insights and understandings of how our minds and bodies work are worth a second read as there really isn't a handbook for the brain out there quite like this."
**Terry Elston, International Corporate Trainer & Author, Trainer of NLP & Hypnosis, www.nlpworld.co.uk**

This book is dedicated to the following:

My Children
My Father
My Friends
L.P
& All Those Who Believed In Me

# How To Change Your Life

## Who am I and What Should I Do with My Life?

Benjamin Bonetti

CAPSTONE
A Wiley Brand

*Registered office*
John Wiley and Sons Ltd, The Atrium, Southern Gate, Chichester, West Sussex, PO19 8SQ, United Kingdom

For details of our global editorial offices, for customer services and for information about how to apply for permission to reuse the copyright material in this book please see our website at www.wiley.com.

*Library of Congress Cataloging-in-Publication Data*

Bonetti, Benjamin, 1982–
  How to change your life : who am I and what should I do with my life / Benjamin Bonetti.
    pages cm
  Includes index.
  ISBN 978-0-85708-464-4 (pbk.)
1. Thought and thinking.   2. Self-actualization (Psychology)   I. Title.
  BF441.B6346 2013
  158–dc23

                                        2013027978

A catalogue record for this book is available from the British Library.

ISBN 978-0-857-08464-4 (paperback)   ISBN 978-0-857-08463-7 (ebk)
ISBN 978-0-857-08462-0 (ebk)   ISBN 978-0-857-08461-3 (ebk)

Cover design by Simon Dovar
Set in 11/14.5 pt Sabon LTStd by Toppan Best-set Premedia Limited
Printed in Great Britain by TJ International Ltd, Padstow, Cornwall, UK

# CONTENTS

# INTRODUCTION

O ver 80 per cent of achievement can be attributed to having the right mind-set. In relation to making changes in your life, having the right mind-set means much more than simply recognizing that change is needed; it means *accepting* that change is always possible, *wanting* to make changes, and *committing* to doing whatever it takes to make those changes happen.

An individual's mind-set can make the difference between achieving their true potential in life or effectively getting stuck in a rut, unable or unwilling to move on from negative experiences that are now holding them back. The contents of this book offer a human engineered MOT, designed to help you identify your current mind-set and get you "on the road" to achieving the life you want.

**The relationship that you hold with yourself determines the path that you will follow.**

As you journey through these pages, you will explore the deep inner values you hold and question the embedded beliefs you have developed based on past experiences, before discovering the world of possibilities that opens up to you simply by learning to use your "true brain" and realizing the optimum ability of the human mind.

Throughout the book, I will be comparing the mental process of change to the physical process of building a temple.

These principles are:

1. The preparation of the foundation – clearing out the old and making way for the new.
2. The selection of materials – obtaining the right tools for the right job.
3. Amending, adapting, planning and visualizing the end result – creating the perfect strategy for your blueprint.
4. Laying the first stone and gaining momentum – building a legacy beyond what you thought was possible.

As listed above, before any building work can begin, the ground must first be cleared in preparation for the setting of a solid foundation. Each new and progressive step in the building process – selecting the material, rounding the edges, setting the stone – can then rest on those firm foundations and a lasting legacy is created.

In addition, throughout each stage you will be asked to complete both tasks and thinking exercises. These have been engineered to trigger new and innovative thinking patterns and reach into the deeper aspects of your subconscious mind to question what you previously thought was possible.

There is a Bible story known as "The Parable of the Two Builders" that Jesus told to drive home the point that listening to his teachings and then ignoring what he said was foolish, like building a house on sand, but listening and then obeying his teachings was wise, like building a house on solid rock. A simplified version of the parable is as follows:

> Two men want to build a house. One man wants the process to be quick and easy so he finds a convenient flat, sandy piece of ground and builds his walls directly on top of it without bothering to do any digging or any other form of preparation. His house was built in no time at all. The other man wants his house to last way beyond his own lifetime so he finds an area of hard ground on which to dig deep foundation trenches for his walls. His house took a long time to build and it was hard work, but it now stands on solid rock beneath the soil.

> Fierce storms raged across the land; strong winds blew and flood waters rose. The house built on solid foundations stood firm but the house built on sand crumbled and was washed away.

So, by likening the process of change to the process of building a temple, you realize that if you want the changes you make to be lasting, you must begin the process by preparing the ground and laying solid foundations: foundations on which you can build a *lasting legacy*.

We live in a culture of "quick fixes" with everything from "buy now, pay later" to the "lose-50-pounds-in-5-minutes-without-exercising-and-eating-as-much-as-you-want" diets on offer. In our heart of hearts we *know* that anything that sounds too good to be true probably is, but the fact remains that many of us are subconsciously drawn in to the belief that we can have whatever we want and we can have it NOW. Of course, when the reality proves not to be quite as *instant* or *effortless* as "promised" we tend to give up on achieving the things we want, sinking into an attitude of "it's too hard; it takes too long; it's not for the likes of me" rather than looking for ways to prepare the ground differently and build stronger, firmer foundations for next time.

*"There are no shortcuts to any place worth going"*
Beverly Sills

The Parable of the Two Builders is as apt in today's world as it was in biblical times. It's a story of attitude and mind-set. The man who built on sand wanted a house, but he wanted the process to be quick and easy – a "quick fix" – so he adopted an attitude of "good enough" rather than one of "is this the best it can be?" His lack of preparation and unwillingness to put in the groundwork led to the efforts he did make being wasted efforts. This rings true for so many people in so many ways today . . . all those who settle for *average*, and all those who give up on achieving what they want at the first obstacle in their path. On the other hand, the man who built on rock also wanted a house, but he wanted a house that *was* the best it could be. Good enough was *not* good enough. He wanted a house that was built to last; a lasting legacy, and he was *committed* to putting in the necessary groundwork to create a solid foundation on which to build it . . . remember, over 80 per cent of achievement can be attributed to having the right mind-set.

My own story is one of building my own lasting legacy. I have journeyed from joining the Army straight out of school to owning several businesses and, over the past decade, personal development has become not only a career but a passion . . . an addiction. I have questioned age old therapies and built a foundation on what I consider to be the most effective tools; tools I have now turned into a change programme that has no name.

**The information contained within this book is only as good as the person who holds it in their hands: the tools provided are only useful if implemented.**

# Step One

# SELECTING THE MATERIAL

"Perfection is achieved, not when there is nothing more to add, but when there is nothing left to take away"
*– Antoine de Saint-Exupéry*

- Is there something that you are struggling to change?
- Are you thinking about a career change perhaps, or a relationship or lifestyle change and you're unsure where to start?
- Could you benefit from a little direction and the kick-start you need?

If you want to change and have decided that enough is enough, then start with **massive action** today.

A definition of massive action:
Taking, not thinking about, but *taking* a focused step
towards achieving your ultimate goal . . . and
following it with another . . .
Massive action = focused action, taken one step at a time.

One thing I decided early on is that we can either change or not: we can continually face obstacles and do nothing about them or we can learn ways to avoid them. Although I am unsure exactly when or where this decision was made, I know that making it has been one of the most influential conscious thinking patterns in my life, and possibly the reason for my success thus far.

How many times have you heard the phrases, "I can't change," or "I don't know where to start," or "It's too hard"? These are incantations we hear every day, all around us, and it begs the question; why do we resist change? Why is it that we resist change and put up with daily difficulties, struggles, and unrest instead: why is it that we put up with these things rather than making changes to create a happier, healthier life? The answer is quite simple; change is misconceived to be difficult. Change is *not* difficult. All it takes is an understanding of *why* you are resisting change and, armed with that understanding, you will be able to change your thinking within a split second, without any conscious thought; and changing your thinking is all it takes to change your world.

So why do we consider change to be so hard? My tried-and-tested theory is that it's not change that is hard but the ability to accept that what was done in the past was not the most beneficial way of doing it. Our biggest psychological challenge is not to change but to accept that the way we have responded to change in the past may not have been the most productive response. Change is a bespoke action. For example, just as we all have different strategies, methods, and approaches to making a cake in order to get the end result we want, the changes *you* need to make are specific to you, your circumstances, and the end result you want. Continuing to do the same things in the same way will bring you the same end results . . . if you want your cake to come out differently, you need to try a different method and approach when making it. Once we have accepted that whether or not to change is a choice, change can become a fluid, conscious choice, not something that happens as a result of pressure, resistance, or the feeling that things have gone on beyond what they should.

> *"You've got a lot of choices.*
>
> *If getting out of bed in the morning is a chore and you're not smiling on a regular basis*
>
> *. . . try another choice"*
>
> Steven D. Woodhull

One thing to accept now is that your subconscious mind has the ability to radically change your thinking patterns through the slightest changes in your everyday language. These slight changes can have consequences that show the power of the human mind and its abilities to adapt to your thoughts. For example, look at the two statements below:

- "I'm going to cut my coffee consumption and drink more water."
- "I'm going to try to cut my coffee consumption and drink more water."

Which statement is most likely to bring the desired outcome? The inclusion of the word "try" in the second statement, although only a slight change, is enough to dilute the power of the statement enormously: either you are going to do it or you are not, *try* is neither one!

> *"Do or do not"* Yoda

When you use the word "try," there's already an expectation of failure in your thoughts. This creates an internal failure state which, when allowed to become the norm, will push your mind to achieve just that – failure.

**Avoid making the assumption that life will not give you what you want or deserve because, in most cases, what you aim to get is exactly what you'll get.**

Making a change can be easy once you know exactly what it is you really want to change, but failure to change can be very much like an internal prison; the real person locked inside, unable to exit, stuck within the boundaries of the body and unable to see the light emanating from the world of opportunities it holds. So how do we change this situation; how do we break out of the prison? The answer lies in changing your view of yourself and the world around you. Just as a prisoner will put pictures of the outside world on their cell wall to remind them of the positive things in their life, your mind will paint and put up pictures of your *perceived* failings on its inner walls to remind you of everything you see as negative in your life, thereby keeping you trapped in that world – unless you change what you see.

## The importance of identity

Answering the question "Who are you?" gives you the material you need to begin laying your rock solid foundations. To give yourself the best possible start, your answer must describe the person you are on the inside, not the physical person others can see on the outside. Knowing who you *really* are, not who you think you *should* be, or who someone else thinks you should be, provides you with the all-important cornerstone on which to build a temple that will last; a lasting legacy.

When we look at some of the most successful people in modern culture, we often gauge their success by their wealth and material possessions. However, if we explore the inner mind of those with a truly remarkable legacy, we discover that their material wealth is merely a by-product of a much deeper, more admirable, attitude and approach to life. My wife and I have often discussed what we would like to leave behind as our lasting legacy, and for us this would not be physical belongings but memories. In our world, the true meaning of success is not found in accumulated material possessions but in the story of our life.

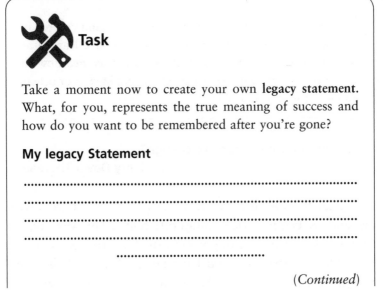

**Task**

Take a moment now to create your own **legacy statement**. What, for you, represents the true meaning of success and how do you want to be remembered after you're gone?

**My legacy Statement**

......................................................................................
......................................................................................
......................................................................................
......................................................................................
..............................................

(*Continued*)

Keep in mind that your legacy may change, and that's fine. Each new stage in your life may change your view of the world around you, but the words you write above must be an accurate reflection of your thoughts and intentions today, now, in this present moment of time.

 **Think . . .**

Think back to the person you were when you were at school . . .

- How did you view the world then?
- How has your view of the world changed since then?

The way you view yourself and the world around you today is based on your past learning. Just as you have learned to read the words on this page, your mind has learned how to read a version of your internal beliefs . . . but have your beliefs about the world changed?

*"Things do not change; we change"*
Henry David Thoreau

As we go through life, our learning processes progress with age and we begin to view things differently. The way you see things is based on the importance of those things to you in your life and the path you have taken. That path is determined by the pictures you have put up on the inner walls of your mind, and those pictures produce the behaviours we see as personality traits. The thoughts you hold in your mind are reflected in your reality, meaning that the person you are on the outside is a direct reflection of the person you are on the inside. Changing the images in your inner world has the power to generate instant changes in your outer world.

*"A man who views the world the same at 50 as he did at 20 has wasted 30 years of his life"*

Muhammad Ali

 **Task**

The next time you are out with friends or meeting someone for the first time, spend a few moments observing not only what they are saying but *how* they are saying it. Around 55 per cent of everyday communication is non-verbal and our body language can speak volumes without saying a word. Pay attention to their behaviours as well as their words and consider how those behaviours may have evolved as a result of their past experiences. Listen also to their words and notice those they say with passion and excitement and those they say with a tone of negativity.

This way of processing a person is something we do every day without conscious thought. It is also the way you communicate with yourself, and it's what makes you strive to change or stay the same. The way you observe others is the way others observe you . . . you can change the way others see you by changing the way you see yourself.

*"To exist is to change, to change is to mature, to mature is to go on creating oneself endlessly"*

Henri Bergson

## Your *world,* your *reality . . . but is it?*

*The way you view yourself and the world around you today is based on your past learning* – this is true, but is *your* view of yourself and your world a *true* view? We all take in information through our senses – sights, sounds, smells, tastes, and sensations – but we don't all take in information from a shared environment or event in the same way. This means that *your* view or experience of an event is not necessarily the same as someone else's view or experience, even when in the same location at the same time. A good example might be the way two people describe a road accident they both witnessed. One person might describe the sounds they heard – the screeching of brakes etc. – while the other might describe the sights they saw – the colours of the cars etc. – and neither one has noticed what the other did, meaning they're unable to verify each other's version of events even though they both witnessed the same accident! We take in information differently so we *experience* things differently. Another example might be the shared experience of a new theme park ride . . . one person might describe the experience as the most exhilarating and fun thing they've ever done, while another might describe it as the most terrifying never-to-be-repeated experience they've ever suffered!

We all take in information from the environment and situation we're in, but we all process it differently. The way we process it is going to influenced by our past experiences; our past *learning*, and this is how we each decide how we're going to think about the experience or how we're going to act in response to the experience. The information we take in is effectively filtered through our existing memories and measured against our established beliefs, values, and attitude to life. We create a picture of the experience in our mind's eye and choose words to internally describe the way we "sensed" it to form an internal representation of the situation or happening in our own mind. In the above theme park example, the person who enjoyed the ride created a positive internal representation based on what they sensed, whereas the person who didn't enjoy the ride created a negative internal representation based on what they sensed. In other words, a positive internal picture of an experience generates positive feel-good emotions, but a negative internal picture generates negative "feel-bad" emotions, and this continues to be the case each time you recall the experience.

Our senses are believed to take in around 2 million bits of information per second, but we can only consciously process around 134 bits of information per second. This means that the huge amount of information we take in every second is being subconsciously filtered to help us sort the information we need to consciously pay attention to at any given moment. The filtering process can be explained through the **NLP Communication Model**:

Deletion – without the ability to delete the information that's of least importance in any given situation, you'd "blow your mind" with an information overload!

Deletion is essentially a process of dropping unnecessary sensory input to a level that your conscious mind can "take in" and manage.

**Distortion** – when we distort information, we effectively "shift" it to create a different version of events or reality; we see things differently. For this reason, distortion plays an important role in allowing us to make "dreams come true" by giving us the imagination and motivation needed to plan ahead and *see* the future we want.

**Generalization** – it's our ability to generalize that allows us to draw enough information from just one or two experiences to come to a general conclusion about any subsequent related experiences. For example, the experience of *not* enjoying one or two theme park rides allows you to make the generalization that you do not like theme park rides! This means that generalization can be an efficient way of learning, but it also means that one experience can be *over* generalized to become a limiting "lifetime" experience; phobias for example.

Each one of us will **delete, distort,** and **generalize** the information we sense at any given time in our own way, explaining why no two people are guaranteed to respond to a shared experience in the same way. *Your* internal representation determines *your* version of events!

## Values, beliefs, and honesty

My father has been a massive influence throughout my life. He is a man who works hard and plays hard; a man who is respected by his friends and family, and a man who overall has many, many good qualities that most aspire to have. His reputation, I believe, is a direct reflection of the man he has become internally. As a role model, he displays the important cornerstone quality of knowing exactly who he is and what he stands for in life, not who he thinks he *should* be. His life has been built around a reality that has turned out to be a direct reflection of the "who" he is rather than the "what" he is.

**Think . . .**

Ask yourself . . .

- **What** have you become?
- **Who** are you to become?

As a parent, it is my job to set ground rules for my children; to teach morals and values, to motivate and support their aspirations, and to fill their heads up with the common knowledge they need for daily living. It is also my job to mould them and guide them in a positive direction.

My wife and I have built a solid foundation for our children in everyday family life by ensuring they have a positive daily routine they can rely on. No parent can teach their child or children everything they need to know in a one-off, one-size-fits-all session, but it's our responsibility as parents to ensure that a progressive learning process is in place, allowing each child to take on board the important principles of life at each new stage of childhood. We help them to build on strong foundations by teaching them right from wrong; teaching them how to behave in different environments; teaching them good manners; teaching them to be respectful of others; and, every bit as importantly, teaching them to respect themselves . . . and we do this by being positive role models ourselves. Children learn by example so it's important that our lead as adults is one that will help them to grow up with the ability to make good decisions for themselves. Of course, children are children, and they can't be expected– nor should they be expected – to behave like adults all of the time. Unacceptable behaviour has consequences, but not all "naughtiness" is deliberate. As parents, we have to make sure our children know what *is* acceptable before reprimanding them for doing otherwise. None of us can know what we don't know . . . until we know!

I see it as extremely important that I remain consistent in my approach to teaching my children the value of life. I give them pep talks on the important aspects of life on a regular and constant basis, and it's through this that we come to understand how our own childhood and past experiences are reflected in our adult lives. Changing our view of ourselves and the world around us today can be a process of stripping back our life and our accumulated belief structure to the basics.

In simple terms, the subconscious mind needs the same careful attention that a parent would give a child. Just as a parent provides shelter, security, nutrition, and positive guidance, the same must be applied to the subconscious. In each case, the positivity in the environment helps to form a solid foundation on which to build.

> *"Be what you are.*
>
> *This is the first step toward becoming better than you are"*
>
> Julius Charles Hare

## *The* real *you* . . .

When defining the real you, and breaking down your real purpose, it's likely that you'll discover a mix of two or perhaps more "people" within a single description. These are the "characters" that make up your personality. However, your mind can become confused when being too many people . . . imagine trying to rehearse for a play and having to remember the scripts for two or three people; how long do you think it would be before the message became jumbled and one turned into the other? Your conscious mind works in a similar way, so it makes sense to simplify things by effectively reducing the number of "characters" you have, combining all of the positive traits in each character to form the true you.

 **Task**

The discovery of the *true you* and the **WHO ARE YOU** . . .

This exercise is designed to utilize and draw together all of the positive traits in each of the different characters currently playing a role in the *whole you* to develop your own "lead character role" as the *true you* . . . the "star" role! Research has shown that personality traits are hereditary, highlighting the importance of identifying and understanding the beliefs you have inherited about yourself and your world.

You may be wondering why it's important to know the one true character of you, but the answer is simply that *character* is what you rely on when facing challenging situations. While it's true that certain aspects of your personality may already shine through under certain circumstances, it's your *true* character that will ultimately carry you and support your change. You only need to think of expressions such as "strength of character" to realize that it takes an understanding of the *true* you – the *real* you – to forge the strength of character you need to know *who* you are and not *what* you are. Unfortunately, most people struggle on through life with too many characters in play, making their character disjointed and unstable, and without any real strength to carry and support them through change.

By combining all of the positive aspects of your separate characters, you define the *true you*:

- Begin by dividing your characters into separate areas on a sheet of paper. So, for example, if you have four distinct characters you would divide your paper into four squares or columns. Make sure you have a big enough sheet of paper to allow room for writing more in each area.

- Now spend five minutes listing all of the positive traits in each of your characters. Remember, this exercise is for *you*, no one else, so write down the positives as *you* see them, not what others may see as a positive in your character. For example:

| SHY | VICTIM |
|---|---|
| Reserved | Non-confrontational |
| Observer | Thinker |
| | Lazy |
| **CONTROLLED** | **DOMINATING** |
| Organised | Winner |
| Methodical | Passionate |
| Stable | Energetic |
| | Intelligent |
| | Engaging |

- Once you have created your lists, draw out a circle and write "True Me" at the top. Spend a further few minutes rewriting the positive traits into the circle and make sure they are exactly how you want to be known – both internally and externally.

You have now collated all of the words that make up the perfect you, so it's time to step into that person; it's time to use the power of **visualization** . . .

- Close your eyes and see yourself in a mirror; as you stare into the mirror, see a reflection of you with all of

*(Continued)*

the traits you have listed in your "true you" circle; notice how you look, how you act, how confident you are, and how you seem to be complete. Notice all of the small things you wouldn't normally notice unless you were *really* looking – there's no rush, so this can take as much time as you need.

- When you are confident that the reflection you see cannot be any better than it is, take a step into it; step into the reflection. As you step in, notice all of the feelings pulsate though your body; experience the emotions unlike any others you have ever felt before, and feel an internal warmth knowing that you have finally found the optimum you: the ***true you***.

- Now spend a few moments visualizing your thoughts and behaviours as the *true you*: notice, internally, how this person . . . this *you* . . . behaves, and notice the benefits that being this *true you* will bring: observe how you will operate within the days, hours, and minutes to come.

## Who decides what you can and can't do?

Our culture has instilled the belief in most of us that success, change, or alternative ways of thinking are beyond our reach. This belief structure became apparent when my son returned home from school one Friday afternoon. During the day's lesson, each of the children had been asked what their parents did for their occupation. Joseph, being just 5 years old at the time, explained that his daddy was a bestselling author and worked with people to make them feel better. Now, not being the stereotypical therapist, I would imagine it difficult on first impression to second guess that as my career choice but, to my amazement, the teacher thought nothing of questioning his answer in a disbelieving manner. After explaining to Joseph that his teacher's response was simply based on her own beliefs about what was possible, and not a representation of what it was possible for him to achieve, I began to think about a way to re-educate and introduce the teacher into the world of possibilities.

That weekend, as part of Joseph's extra-curricular activities, we set about producing his very own self-published book. It took only two weeks for the first draft copy to arrive and, after taking it into his school, Joseph was presented with an award for creativity. He deserved it; but as parents, it is our duty to encourage our children to challenge the beliefs of others and not to accept the limitations of others as their own. We must all discover our own limitations for ourselves. I share this story not just to prove how strongly we are controlled by our limitations, but to show how powerful our restrictions can be if we make a conscious choice to accept our path and fail to alter it for the better. Who knows, Joseph's teacher could have a bestselling book of her own hidden away within her mind . . .

## Accepting risk and failure

The most common reason why many people fail to change is that they fail to lay their first brick: they stop, often with brick in hand. You only need one brick to start building but building can only begin when you lay it.

So what is stopping you from changing?

- ... too much hard work?
- ... not enough time?
- ... pure laziness?
- ... or the fear of failing; *your* failing?

Failing to lay the first brick is failing to take massive action; it's failing to make the essential differences in your life that will give you the solid foundations you need to begin building the life you want. The longer you fail to make those differences, the longer you will carry around with you a sense of being unfulfilled each and every day. Life is a self-fulfilling prophecy: the more *you* change, the more the change in your life; the more you stay the same, the more of that very same you will enjoy!

Just as a building planner looks at the potential of a piece of land and builds an image of the completed project in their mind, your success can be visualized in the same way at this foundation stage. You can create a mental image of your finished temple, your legacy, and you can begin to draft the plans. Just as the project manager on a building site needs a detailed step-by-step plan to build upwards from foundations, you need your own detailed plans to follow to get you from where you are now to where you want to be.

However, if you have ever watched any property building or renovation programmes on TV, you will know that things don't always go to plan ... projects rarely get finished within the predicted time frame, and they invariably come in way over budget. But, in the majority of cases, they *do* get finished. The people in question *lay the first brick* and the process of building their dream begins. Now imagine what would happen if those same people started out with thoughts of "What if it all goes wrong?" or, "What if we've made a mistake in our plans?" What would happen is – nothing! The first brick would never be laid and their dream home would remain nothing more than a muddy field and some drawings on paper. Laying the first brick means accepting that there are risks and that things *could* go wrong but, crucially, it also means accepting that just because things could go wrong, it doesn't mean they *will*. There are no guarantees, but one thing that is *for sure* is that if they don't lay the first brick, their dream cannot become a reality.

Of course, those who succeed are those who build onto rock solid foundations, not sand, but also those who have the right mind-set as they lay the first brick. Without the right mind-set, the first hiccup in the building process is likely to lead to tools being put down and everything on-site grinding to a halt. As the tools go down, thoughts of, "This is too hard," or, "This is never going to be finished," take over, meaning that the project may be abandoned totally or an attitude of corner-cutting and "good enough" slips in. Either way, the end result is that every effort is effectively a wasted effort.

> *"If a job is worth doing, it's worth doing well"*
> Proverb

The potential to fail only exists because the potential to succeed also exists. With the right mind-set, thoughts of,

"What if this doesn't go to plan," can be replaced with thoughts of, "What if this *does* go to plan." If you are able to focus your thoughts on failure and create a mental image of what that failure will look like for you, you are also able to switch your thoughts to focus on success and create a mental image of what that success will look like for you.

It's the *vision* of a successful build that keeps a project manager on track to achieving it. Each step of the building process is planned, but it's *accepted* that things don't always go to plan. With a clear image of the desired finished project in mind, a project manager can deal with building hiccups as and when they occur, and create a new plan to get from where the hiccup has taken them to where they want to be . . . and can still get to, *if* they keep their tools in hand.

## Stepping stones . . .

Planning and visualizing your success could be termed by some individuals as setting yourself a goal. In the building example above, it's the project manager's *goal* to create a finished building that looks exactly like the architect's drawings. He has a clear image of the finished project in mind, so he has clear goal to aim for. However, I am not a great fan of goals for the simple reason that goals seem so terminal! There's a finality about goals that suggests once they've been achieved, that's it – job done. For me, it's not about the destination, it's about the journey . . . it's all about the legacy.

Of course, we all need points of reference to aim for in order to know we're heading in the right direction, but I choose not to refer to those points as goals. The problem with goals is that you can set them and then *not* achieve them, and I struggle to see where this type of premeditated failure can be of benefit to you on your journey towards success. Your journey will always be on track if you are congruent in your intent and your actions. To build a lasting legacy you must learn from your past, prepare for your future, and, most importantly, live in the present by doing your best at any given moment . . . but more on this later. For now, the process of building begins by laying the first brick and then laying the next, and the next. For this reason, and for the purposes of this book, I'm choosing to use the term stepping stones rather than goals. Stepping stones keep you moving . . . and movement is exactly what you need. Remember, it's all about the journey, not the destination, and when you have stepping stones, you can keep on journeying across a never ending pool of water – there is no *one* destination to reach.

 **Think . . .**

Take a moment to think about the following and come up with your own answers . . .

### Diets never work – why?

My answer is as follows: diets never work because individuals set themselves a goal, and once they achieve that goal, they revert back to their previous bad habits. The goal becomes a

*(Continued)*

destination, and arrival at that destination signals *job done* and a return to old ways.

### Legacies work – why?

My answer is as follows: legacies work because choosing to leave a legacy represents a lifestyle choice; and every change remains a lasting change because each one forms an integral link in your on-going journey.

### New Year's resolutions don't work – why?

My answer is as follows: New Year's resolutions fail because they have no longevity. They are target (destination) driven as opposed to lifestyle driven. And, if you're really honest with yourself, what is it about January 1 that makes you think change will magically happen on that date? Why not the June 5, or the November 8; why not NOW?

## You're already there . . .

When you learn to visualize yourself standing on each new stepping stone on your journey, you learn how to get into **the state of already having**. This is a great tool to use when you want to change mental aspects of your behaviour, meaning your attitude and the way you think about things. Getting into the state of already having allows you to experience the "reality" of being the person you will become as you reach each stepping stone and having or doing the things each stepping stone represents. You *already have it* so you can experience the thoughts and emotions of being there; you can take in the view of the world you now have as you look out from the new vantage point.

The concept is simply that if you want something, it's useful to get into a state that reflects already having the something you want. However, a word of warning: getting into the state of already having is an effective *mental* exercise and should not be taken literally as a physical exercise. For example, if you want a supercar but can't afford one, avoid going out and getting one to experience the physical state of *already having*. You see, no amount of positive thinking or visualization is going to change the way the finance company sees things – and it's unlikely that the finance company will accept your explanation of "just getting into the state"!

## How's the view?

A vision board is a great way to remind yourself of the *true you* and also the person you are to become. Remember, perfection is not found in having nothing more to add but in having nothing left to take away, and your vision board should represent the *nothing left to take away* version of you and your life. Everything on your board must be positive . . . a reminder of what you want, not what you *don't* want. The images on your vision board represent the view of yourself and the world you will see as you stand on each stepping stone, and looking at those images is a great way to get into the mental state of already having.

## Task

Make it a daily ritual to look at your vision board and visualize the life you will have as a result of your change. This is something that can be done first thing every morning or last thing at night, and it can even be done as you sit on the train on your way to work. Taking the time to visualize your life in this way is an effective way to remind yourself of who you are to become and experience the state of already having.

## *All change . . .*

Being able to experience a state of already having is a powerful tool to have in your "tool kit" and being able to *change* your state whenever you choose to is equally powerful. Throughout the course of a normal day, your state is more than likely changed by certain *triggers* that you may not even be aware of. For example, there may be a certain piece of music that can instantly change your emotional state when you hear it; the music is the trigger that changes your state. This is something that the producers of "music for exercise" MP3s and DVDs use to full advantage by selecting "high energy" tracks that inspire listeners and viewers to get active . . . and buy into more of their products!

Your task is to discover the triggers that generate a positive emotional change in you. Whether it's a music track or an image on your vision board, you need to identify the triggers that allow you to move away from a negative state and return to a positive, vibrant, and energetic state. From this point forward, this positive state is going to be known as your *true state* and finding the triggers that put you in it will allow you to get into it whenever you face a situation that requires focus, strength, and clarity. Your triggers must be things that generate a positive change in your state every time, without fail, and it's knowing what those triggers are that allows you to keep moving forwards when things are not going to plan. Your triggers effectively help to prevent you from putting down your tools when thoughts of "This is too hard" enter your mind.

## *States strategy . . .*

As humans we are built in a way that leads to us being the most resourceful we can be at any one time.

The different states are:

- **Action State** – this is your adrenaline rush; your super state! It's in your action state that you make the most radical changes as it's in this state that you are likely to take action outside of your usual character. For example, this could be committing to a parachute jump even though you have a fear of heights or of flying, or perhaps standing up to someone who would normally intimidate you.
- **Sleepy State** – this is your Friday afternoon state! It's in this state that you just want to relax and sit down;

you are looking forward to simply doing nothing, perhaps opening a bottle of wine, ordering a takeaway, and generally zoning out. This state is the ideal state for recharging your mind.

- **Thinking State** – this is your lost in thought state; a state in which your mind wanders and minutes can turn into hours. This state is usually reserved for reflection and methodical thinking.
- **Parental State** – you don't need to have children to adopt this state! It's in this state that you start to think about changes in your career, relationships, or any other significant elements of your life. This state involves a lot of internal talk and generally an internal questioning and answering process.
- **Relaxed State** – this state is usually only achieved when you spend a period of time outside of your usual environment. For example, it usually takes a few days of holiday time to *truly* unwind and get into a relaxed state, but you can also experience this state through short bursts of deep relaxation, or during massage or hypnosis.
- **Dancing State** – this is your "just want to let my hair down" state! This state is usually experienced after a stressful time, and when pent up energy is bursting to get out.

Take a few moments to think about the above states and how each one might affect your day to day life. Recognizing the different states makes it possible to begin changing your state to adopt the frame of mind that will be of most benefit to you at any given point in your day . . . and on your journey.

## Getting into state

You can get into any state you *choose* – you just need to decide which state it is you wish to anchor. Be clear on the reasons *why* you want to recall this state and then accept that once triggered, it may be hard to change.

 **Task**

List the reasons *why* you want to want to trigger this behavioural state, including all of the positive benefits it will bring. It's important to use positive words, focusing on what you want *not* what you don't want.

- Go back in time in your mind and think of a situation or event in which you experienced the state you want to recall. Remember the way you felt; what could you see, hear, smell, and taste . . . relive *every* detail but avoid focusing on variables such as the weather conditions or the ages of the individuals in the images you create.
- Now list everything you remember about what happened. How did you feel before, during, and after the event? Be specific; the specific emotions or feelings will become your strategies for recalling this state. If you have more than one situation or event in mind, duplicate the process and run them in parallel.
- It's now time to think about the state *trigger* – the visual or kinaesthetic reminder that triggers the state

*(Continued)*

35

response. It's worth noting that you will have a preferred trigger aid. For example, if you use phrases such as, "Did you see that?" or "Seeing is believing," then you will likely find it more beneficial to use a visual trigger. If you find yourself using phrases such as, "That felt amazing" or "I won't believe it until I touch it," then it's likely that you will benefit from touching something to trigger a response.

A good friend and mentor once told me, "The power is within the red dot," so finding your trigger is finding your own red dot . . . or your own "lucky foot"! However, it's important to think ahead. Make sure your trigger is something that's appropriate for use in public places or in controlled environments such as business meetings . . . not everyone will be comfortable with the appearance of a lucky foot! Utilize objects you would normally carry around with you or things that wouldn't look out of place. For example, a good friend of mine uses gum to trigger his action state.

- Now rewind the event and double-check that you have listed all of the exact feelings and emotions; start to add more life to the event by adding more detail about what you saw, heard, smelled or tasted as appropriate. Allow any emotions to flow, perhaps allowing your eyes to close for a moment as you enjoy the powerful recollection.
- As you flow through the event, notice the starting point of the state, the peak point, and the point at which it begins to reduce.

  This – led to – this – led to – this – led to –
  this – peak – led to – this . . .

- Follow this process again; flow through the event again and notice the key points of build-up and peak. As you reach the emotional peak this time, **look at** or **touch** the trigger.
- Repeat a further five times until the trigger is embedded within your neurology; repetition is an essential part of the exercise.

Once you have completed this task, it's time to test how effective your trigger has become. But, before you do, spend a moment away from the triggered state – perhaps read the last line backwards or do anything mundane that will break the wanted state.

- **Test your trigger** – now you have set the trigger, it's time to fire it! Take two deep breaths then fire your visual or kinaesthetic trigger. As you do so, notice how quickly your body can return to the desired positive state.

To push this exercise further, or to intensify the experience, you can stack the anchors. The principle is the same but rather than listing the emotions from one event, use the trigger for a number of events or situations in which you experienced similar (as close as possible) emotional strengths.

## Actions speak louder than words . . .

On the subject of triggers, it's worth noting that affirmations are commonly promoted as a way of changing your state. An internal chant of "I can do this" or "I am a winner" *can* bring about a positive change in state, but an affirmation can only ever be effective when it's said with a purpose. When Andy Murray became the first British male Grand Slam tennis champion for 76 years, in 2012, he admitted to "having a word with himself" in the restroom mirror when he took a mid-match comfort break! He looked at himself in the mirror and told himself that he could win. His words focused his mind on what he wanted and what he was going to go back out and *do* to get what he wanted. This form of affirmation can, and did, promote a positive result, but it must be noted that the words spoken were said with the purpose of promoting positive *actions*. Great care must be taken to avoid incantations that focus on what you *don't* want.

## Select the right ground on which to build your foundation

Remember, *making a change can be easy once you know exactly what it is you really want to change.* When you recognize the *true you*, you also recognize the changes you need to make to create the life you really want.

> **Your commitment to change is your commitment to having a better life.**

We can complain about many things that appear to be fixed, but are your current circumstances *really* fixed? Are you *really* stuck with the life you have rather than the life you want? When you recognize your *true state*, you recognize the things that inspire you in life; the things you feel passionate about, and the things that generate a positive change in your emotional state. If your current circumstances are *not* conducive to being in your true state, are you *really* unable to change them?

For example, let's say you currently live in a rural area and you now recognize that it's being in the heart of a busy city that brings you to life – or vice versa. Now, I recognize that upping sticks and moving is not always an easy option, and that having children in school or a partner in employment creates many restrictions and limitations, but if you recognize it as a move that would improve your current life, what is there to stop you looking into the steps you would need to take to be able to make the giant leap? There is *nothing* to stop you, only your own imagined fears . . . *what if it doesn't work out; what if I fail?*

This brings us full circle to the question asked earlier: **what is stopping you from changing?**

- . . . too much hard work?
- . . . not enough time?
- . . . pure laziness?
- . . . or the fear of failing; *your* failing?

Why not turn your focus around and question what would happen if you couldn't fail: what if you only achieved the best for you, and what if life was planned to give you all the successes you deserve?

Recognizing what you want to change is the first step towards making that change. Someone once said to me . . .

If you live life to achieve a good life, you'll get an okay life; if you live life to achieve a great life, you'll achieve a good life; if you live life to achieve an awesome life, you'll achieve a great life.

You, and only you, can set the bar in terms of how you're going to live your life. Remember, knowing who you *really* are gives you the material you need to begin laying your rock solid foundations. You are not the person you thought you were; you are a lot more than that. It's a common misconception that we are simply the person we are seen as on the outside, and we're generally measured by the wealth of our belongings – or the "*what*" we are rather than the "*who*" we are – but true wealth can only ever be truly measured by the thoughts and the smile you can produce on the inside.

## Selecting the material checklist

- ☐ Commit to taking **massive action**
- ☐ Accept that change is a choice
- ☐ Accept that things do not always go to plan
- ☐ Identify the *true you*
- ☐ Identify your *true state* triggers
- ☐ Choose to focus on the journey, not the destination

# Step Two
# ROUNDING THE EDGES

"Best is good. Better is best"

*– Lisa Grunwald*

## *The better you see life, the better life will be . . .*

Your mental attitude towards change or any other task is the difference between success and failure. By looking at a task with a positive mind-set, you change the dynamics of your thinking and physiology . . . for the better.

Even very small changes to your building blocks can make big changes to the structure of your building . . . and its ability to withstand the test of time.

## A different approach

Creating a different culture and attitude to change begins with your family and those closest around you. All it takes is a small change, but a change made with commitment is a change that can begin in a small minority and spread with a ripple effect to positively influence the majority.

 **Think . . .**

Follow the simple exercise below to discover how "thinking" alone can massively change your outcomes. Before you begin, take a moment to think about where your positive emotions come from; think about a positive event or a happy loving face . . . and as you do, take a snapshot of your internal emotions and begin to identify where those feelings originate in your body. Now follow the same process but with thoughts of a negative event . . . and identify where those feelings originate.

Armed with a greater awareness of where positive or negative feelings originate in your body, think about the following:

- Think of an event that in the past would have created a negative feeling; perhaps a meeting with a certain person, visiting a particular environment, or something you recognize as creating negative emotions.
- As you do so, begin to notice all of the smaller points in your snapshot and start to change them in whatever way you can – perhaps changing the colour, changing certain movements, or changing the sounds. Through this process you can repaint your snapshot picture and also change the emotions you feel when you look at it.
- As you repaint your picture, start to smile and begin to change the direction of the emotions within your body. For example, if you have identified that your feelings are rotating from right to left in an anti-clockwise movement, switch the movement to rotate your feelings

in a clockwise movement. With practice, you can push this exercise a little further by beginning to move the emotions you feel to another part of your body.

- Notice how the intensity and direction of the movement change the dynamics of the emotion. If you are able to move the emotions to a different area of your body, you can repeat the exercise to move them again to another location, thereby changing the properties of that event or experience once more.

I have used this process with many of my clients, especially those who have issues with past events. Remember, the past offers nothing more or nothing less than the knowledge of how to do something differently: you can't change the past but you can learn more about what to do next time.

Being able to look at an event differently is not only a useful tool; it's a fantastic method of alternative learning. As humans, we take in information via our five senses – sight, sound, smell, taste, and touch – and it's through the senses that strategies are formulated based on our previous learning. Our behaviours are the result of our learned strategies. However, anything that can be learned can also be *un-learned:* you can learn how to re-present information.

## Representation = to Re – Present

When you re-present a situation you have the ability to change the behaviour. Try the following simple exercise to experience for yourself how easy it can be to bring about change.

**Task**

- Take a moment to think about the clothes you wore this morning. When you do this, notice how you effectively go inside your mind and either see yourself wearing the clothes or see the clothes before you put them on. You are able to do this by being able to visualize the past and make an internal representation about the event.

- Now think about the top you wore. Change the colour to bright yellow . . . canary yellow . . . the brightest yellow you have ever seen! Notice how your internal feelings change as you do this. In what way would wearing the bright yellow top alter your thinking about the day? Would you smile more, or just stand out more? How would this feel? In what ways would you feel different?

By utilizing this powerful technique you can represent the past in a completely different way. The above exercise demonstrates how you can use colour to change what you see but you can change any of the sensory inputs to change sounds, smells, tastes, and textures. It's an exercise that you can really have fun with. For example, try touching a glass of cold water but tell yourself it's hot . . . notice the learned behaviour changes!

## *Modelling*

Through my work over the years, and even prior to my therapy profession, I was always interested in learning about people who, despite being subjected to the most horrific of circumstances, somehow managed to come through it all and radically change their life.

There are many real-life inspirational stories to choose from, but there is one particular story that has always stayed with me. It's the story of Jozef Paczynski, a Polish Political Prisoner and survivor of Auschwitz. In a documentary of his story, he describes the living conditions and the internal prisoner policies within the quarters. He calmly paints a picture of what his everyday life was like and the mind-set he adopted . . .

> *"These things couldn't be helped, in other words don't think about it, it's been and gone.*
>
> *We had to think about where to go to work, to survive the following day, to watch your bread so that nobody stole it . . . so you could have breakfast and go to work to find a lighter job, this is what you were preoccupied with.*
>
> *This was a constant vigilance, be vigilant, you have to survive."*

When you look at the words he uses and dissect the actions he took, it demonstrates the "survivor" within us. He refuses to dwell on the past; he accepts that some external actions are out of his control and, as unimaginably horrific as it was, he made the choice to take every day as it came – one day at a time. Jozef looked after what was important and let everything else pass by.

I think that a lot can be learned from those who are pushed to the extremes, whether the extremes are forced upon them or taken by choice. When you take on board the amazing feats of internal bravery shown by some individuals, you learn that the mind is more than just the physical body, and much more than the words that are said.

## Conscious and subconscious training . . .

The difference between the conscious and subconscious mind can be explained as follows:

> You are **consciously** reading this sentence.
> You are **subconsciously** attaching meaning to
> the words in these sentences.

The conscious mind and subconscious mind are very different, but equally important in terms of learning how to train your mind. Your **conscious** mind (conscious thinking) is the part of the mind that works out the present thinking; it's the analytical part, dealing with the bits of information that need your immediate attention. It is said that this part of the mind can only process up to nine bits of information at any one time. Your **subconscious** mind (subconscious thinking) is the part of your mind that works out the inner you; it's the part that controls your micro movement and the general maintenance of your body – effectively guiding your body through each of the steps required for everyday functioning on "auto pilot" setting. In comparison to the conscious mind, the subconscious mind can process thousands of bits of information at any one time.

To train your mind, attempt to take up both your internal and your external thinking simultaneously. For example:

- Sit at your computer and type out a well-known story; a story you know "off by heart," while simultaneously watching a film on TV.
- To do this, you must be looking at the TV and not your computer screen, therefore you are touch-typing the story.
- Maintain an awareness of your breathing and attempt to type out the story without allowing thoughts of what you are watching or thinking to interrupt your writing.

The above exercise can be a lot of fun to try but there is a serious aspect to it in that it re-sets the connection between conscious and subconscious thought. By overloading your five senses with simultaneous actions, you calibrate not only the senses but also your mind.

## Educating your past

*"We are made wise not by the recollection of our past, but by the responsibility for our future"*
George Bernard Shaw

### *Be responsible for your own actions . . .*

Responsibility is a harder trait to achieve than most people think, but it's the cornerstone to building the perfect temple and the legacy that you leave.

The challenge is to take responsibility for "all" of your actions, but by taking responsibility for your actions you free your mind from the choice of error. Errors only occur when responsibility is subconsciously given away. If you make the choice to take responsibility for *everything* you do, each consequence of your actions will be emotionally free; and by being responsible for your actions, it means there is limited opportunity for errors to occur.

It is impossible for errors to occur if you purposely intend to take responsibility for the result of that action. Here's a simple example: imagine asking a friend to help you decide which outfit you should wear to a special occasion. If it turns out that you feel over or under dressed when you get there, you "blame" your friend for making you feel that way . . . you subconsciously gave away responsibility and your negative emotions are a consequence.

 **Task**

Your thoughts and actions today and every day, create the person you are tomorrow and in the future. With this in mind, take just a few minutes every day to think about being responsible for your thoughts; make the choice to alter any negativity in your thoughts or in your behaviours as those thoughts and actions may make you responsible for being someone you want to avoid being!

Taking just a few moments to consciously take responsibility on a daily basis can bring about exciting changes. You will be able to transform your life and make responsible decisions based on a state that supports a positive outcome, because each choice you make will be the result of a positive thought process or behaviour.

Get excited about the person you will be tomorrow and in the future as a result of changing the way you think and act today. By visualizing the end result, even if a lifetime away, you provide your mind with much needed focus and direction. The changes you make today are the rounding of the edges that will help you to build a lasting legacy.

## You always have a choice . . .

The way you choose to think about a particular happening or react to it is exactly that – a choice. There are no "good" or "bad" choices to be made, only choices, and each choice is made in just one moment of time. If the choice you make proves not to bring you the end result you wanted, you're not all out of choices – choose again, but choose to do things differently. Remember, you can't change what has already happened, but you can learn more about what to do next time, and when you take responsibility for the choices you make, you limit the potential for errors to occur.

**Follow through on your choices every time . . . solid choices make solid foundations.**

As a country lover, being in busy, built-up areas feels alien to me, but I sometimes have to make a trip into London. When this is the case, I choose to get in and out as quickly as possible. I may not have a choice over whether or not to go into London, but I can choose how I think about it and how I do it. Choosing to get in and out quickly is a choice based on my own personal experience of where I am most productive and where I am able to function at my peak. Recognizing where you feel your "best self" is an important step towards making choices that can radically change your life for the better.

*"Life is the sum of all your choices"*

Albert Camus

## Forgiving and letting go

Having gone through many struggles in my own life, I have learned that although the future can appear bleak at times and any hope of a happier future can appear unreachable, the reality is that the future you want is just a few steps away with a little more persistence and patience. However, it is during those final few steps before achieving the change you want that you are most likely to begin focusing on and reminding yourself of past failures or obstacles. This form of self-sabotage can often be the most damaging as it produces an ever-growing list of irrational reasons for *not* continuing with the process of change.

*"I'm building up my problems to the size of a cow"*

The Wonder Stuff

## *Facing fear . . .*

The fear of the unknown is perhaps one of the most commonly spoken about fears, and it's described as the single most-used reason people give for failing to make changes. Unfortunately, for most of those who fail to make changes, the life they are currently living is not the life they have in reality – it's a lot worse. I have been guilty of this in past, especially when facing some of the most challenging of times, and it's essentially a case of playing down the real situation. It's perhaps something we're all guilty of at times, but we can choose to fake a clear future by creating false affirmations that things will somehow magically get better or we can choose to take massive action and make the changes that will make things better. Choosing to adopt an attitude of "things will get better" can be detrimental to the overall objective and it's a "head in the sand" approach that will affect the stability of your legacy from the foundations upwards.

The "fake truth" is something we have all no doubt told ourselves at least once in our lifetime. It's a process of self-justification and of playing down a personal issue by comparing it to someone else who has the same issue but to a much greater extreme. The "fake truth" acts as a buffer to the *actual* truth and generates an attitude of "Things are not that bad," allowing you to slip into an "It's going to get better" state. However, once you adopt this state, you're on a slippery slope, and each time you repeat the negative affirmations, you reaffirm your acceptance of the "fake truth" as being the *actual* truth.

## *Are you carrying excess baggage?*

Okay, while it's true that we can all learn from the past and utilize our experiences, we cannot trust the past to be absolute truth. You only need to consider the enormous amount of learning that goes on between birth and teenage years to realize the potential for truth to be stretched and diluted, and for inaccuracies to be taken as facts.

> *"When I was a boy of fourteen, my father was so ignorant I could hardly stand to have the old man around. But when I got to twenty-one, I was astonished by how much he'd learned in seven years"*
>
> Mark Twain

Of course, it's within these early formative years that your values and beliefs are formed, and these can have both a positive and negative effect on your life. However, you always have a choice: you can choose which beliefs to keep and which to discard at any point in your life. For this reason, learning to recognize the values and beliefs that support you and those that don't is a sensible place to begin in terms of identifying where changes can be made for the better.

 **Task**

Take a pen and paper and write down the values and beliefs you currently hold. This doesn't need to be an exhaustive list, just the ones that come readily to mind. For example, "I value family life" or "I believe in ghosts." Next, draw a line down the centre of another sheet of paper and give one side the heading "keep" and the other side the heading "discard." Go through your list of values and beliefs and decide which side of the paper each one should be placed. Rewrite each one in the chosen column. The use of the word "chosen" here is important, as a value or belief, no matter how unsupportive it may be in your life, can only be discarded when *you* choose to do so.

The values and beliefs you hold are effectively the infrastructure of your life; they are the blueprint. They offer you control over when to take action and when to let things pass you by, and thereby dramatically affect the life you lead. I am a great believer that we are all born with the same blueprint, and we all have an equal share in what the world will allow us to do . . . based on our future actions.

I remember being in a hole some years back. I had no money, I had just separated from my wife, and my life was generally not going in the right direction. After a bit of self-pity and self-realization, I put the whole situation into perspective. It all comes down to knowing what's important to you. I can now list no more than five things that are *truly* important to me. It's personal, but knowing what they are puts any failure or setback into an altogether easier to swallow "dose"!

 **Task**

Write out your own list of things that are *truly* important to you, and limit it to no more than five things.

## *Use reflection to see your future . . .*

Wallowing in self-pity may be something we need to go through in order to reach a point of self-realization, but it's not a productive state to hang around in for too long. However, reflective meditation can be a powerfully productive tool to use when you need to think about the direction your life is heading and the alterations you need to make to get yourself back on track to achieving the life you want.

Reflective meditation should be a peaceful time that's free of distractions, both external and internal, and your thoughts should be focused only on reflecting on your journey so far. The question you must ask yourself is . . .

- . . . Where are you on your current path to achievement?

And, if life is not going in the direction you want it to, ask yourself this . . .

- . . . Who is going to make the changes needed to change direction?

Of course, there can be times when we reach a point of thinking that things look so bad they couldn't possibly get any worse. When this is the case, they probably will! But, as the great Winston Churchill once said, "We must just KBO." The initials KBO stood for "Keep Buggering On."

There are two types of people in this world; the talkers and the doers. But once all of the talking is done, it is left to the doers to do what they do best – change the world.

## Which one are you . . . a talker or a doer?

When you make the choice to change, you must commit to making that change. When you *talk* about making changes, there's an inherent danger that you'll slip back into the patterns and habits that led to you *thinking* and *talking* about making changes in the first place. Resistance is needed to *question* your values – it is not there to stop you from making those positive intentions a reality by taking massive action.

## Take a load off . . .

Forget the past, all it offers is baggage. As children, we all had people we modelled, so what we must now do is return to that same starting point; that same beginning where we effectively had a clean slate on which to begin our learning, and we began to create an imprint of the person we would become as adults.

Whether you were bullied at school or you were a grade "A" student, the input from the outside world via your senses has determined who you are, and continues to be an important aspect of your subconscious programming; this is something I call unconscious conditioning. Any event that is persistently experienced will start to fix a blueprint into your hardwiring. Just as physical repetition can make a well-practised task fluid, and something you are able to do without consciously thinking about it, your mind will adopt the same response to repetitive thoughts and actions related to your values and beliefs. This means it's not the external information we have to control, but rather the choices we make – and the internal blueprint this creates within our minds.

Treasure what's important to you and let everything else pass you by. Think about what *really* counts and make a choice to delete the rest. As part of your change, make an effort to remove any useless baggage.

## Enough is enough . . . the "ah ha" moment!

There comes a point when enough is enough, and through pain or otherwise, you become motivated enough to take action . . . to make the choice to change and to never look back. For most people, this "ah ha" moment only comes when the pain of the issue becomes too much to endure for a moment longer, but it doesn't have to be this way. Strange as it may seem, the sense of familiarity and certainty an issue creates in someone's life can effectively lead to them continuing to repeat the same actions in order to remain in the same familiar situation. The certainty of knowing is somehow "safer" than the uncertainty of letting go . . . but you can let go of pain or any other negative emotion at *any* time.

The **white cloud** technique is something I use with clients who have emotions, fears, and issues in their past that they want to let go of. It's a very simple exercise that revolves around inducing a trance-like state using visualization techniques, but it has proven to have a big impact in terms of effectiveness across the board. Clients using this technique have found the internal motivation required to finally let go . . . forever.

 ## The White Cloud

This exercise is best completed just before going to bed at night. Find yourself a comfortable place to sit or lie down and ensure that you will not be disturbed. Some people find it helps to create a calming ambiance by lighting a candle and listening to gentle, relaxing music. The steps involved will need to be memorized, so read through the following information several times before putting the steps into practice – or, alternatively, you could make an audio recording using your own words. The induced trance-like state is completely safe and you will be able to awaken immediately whenever you need to.

Before you begin, decide which negative thoughts you want to let go of and identify the associated sub-modalities. In NLP, the senses (sight, sound, smell, taste, and touch) are known as modalities and sub-modalities provide the finer details. For example, you may see a colour – is it bright or faint? You may hear a sound – is it loud or muffled? You may feel a particular sensation – is it in a particular location in your

*(Continued)*

body; is it warm or cold? Make a list of every sub-modality associated with the thought you want to let go of. This allows you to create an internal representation of the "experience" and once you have that clear internal vision, you can begin the following step-by-step process:

1.  Relax; turn off any distractions and just lie or sit still for a moment listening to your breathing.
2.  Gently rotate your neck, your arms, your legs, and your feet.
3.  Smile, and move your jaw from side to side.
4.  Take a deep breath and close your eyes.
5.  Just breathe for a few minutes, listening to your breath and the way that you breathe
6.  Start to notice how one part of your body seems to become warmer than the other . . . then how the warmth starts to move around your body, relaxing each part of it as it does. Perhaps relaxing a little more with every outward breath.
7.  When you feel that your whole body has relaxed and is comfortably warm, start to notice any thoughts you had before just drifting away . . . not knowing where they are going, but just accepting that they can leave.
8.  Now, as you rest, start to relax a little more.
9.  Notice the deep blue warming sky above, and how its warmth penetrates each of the nerves, fibres, and muscles within your body.
10. Now begin to notice a white cloud appearing, drifting down and immersing you.
11. Notice the slight chill on your skin, and as you become immersed, allow it to push . . . *whichever*

*sub-modalities you listed* . . . out of your body, through your pores.

12.   As the cloud rises, you notice how the cloud removes and takes with it the concerns, attachments, emotions, thoughts, and previously triggered actions with it.

13.   Drift and relax; notice how the feelings in your body are positively different. You perhaps feel a little lighter.

14.   As the cloud drifts away, you notice a smile appearing as it takes with it any remaining negative associations.

15.   As you look up for the final time, notice how the cloud has gone completely.

16.   Relax for a few moments and enjoy this state of freedom.

This exercise can be altered along with the environment, and you can create a place where you feel comfortable to allow your changes to happen. You might choose to push the previous issue further away until it has gone completely, or to change the sub-modalities and the feelings associated with them.

There may also be times you feel angry about an event, situation, or person but fail to remember the actual reason! When this is the case, any details you do remember are likely to have become **distorted** and therefore they are no longer a reliable source of information on which to base your real reason for holding on to feelings of anger. Either way, it's time to let go.

> *"You've got to accentuate the positive, eliminate the negative . . ."*
> Ac-cent-tchu-ate The Positive, Harold Arlen, Johnny Mercer (1944)[1]

You might instantly recognize the above song lyrics, but whether or not you know the tune, the message contained in the words makes the song worthy of a listen. A fundamental part of change is recognizing the language we use and the way in which we use it. Many people face issues and seek change in life, not because they have made the "wrong" decisions, but because they have viewed the outcomes of their decisions in the wrong manner. One of the main reasons for this lies in the words we use; the language we use in our internal dialogue, and the "story" we tell ourselves about the event or happening. For example, imagine you've just tried a new recipe for the first time and the end result is not looking anything like the picture in the book! You say to yourself "I don't know why I even bother. I'm a hopeless cook and nothing ever works out the way it's meant to," or words to that effect. However, the story you're telling yourself is not the whole story. Yes, the recipe you've just tried may have ended in disaster but you've actually been feeding your family delicious meals all week without any complaints. You are in fact a *good* cook and your willingness to have a go with new recipes is what keeps you moving forwards to becoming an even better cook. Of course, the use of words such as "hopeless" and telling yourself that things "*never* work out" leads

[1] *Ac-cent-tchu-ate The Positive* reproduced from Johnny Mercer Song Database (2004), Popular Music Collection, Special Collections Department, Georgia State University Library.

to negative thoughts and beliefs about yourself and your abilities in the kitchen.

Along with your internal voices, you will also use a number of pre-programmed words that you have given a prior meaning. It's my belief that it takes just a few alterations to the words you use to bring about radical and immediate changes. To intensify an event, you can simply change the dynamics of the words you use to describe it. As another example, imagine you wake up one morning and discover it's snowing outside. Do you instantly look at the negatives or the positives?

 **Think . . .**

- Do you use negative language to describe the situation?
- Or do you smile and use a description that generates a positive feeling about the situation?

Slipping into the unproductive state of using negative language is usually something that happens on a subconscious level, but by being aware of the language you are using and by making others aware of your intention to change it, you can soon bring about the subconscious change needed to alter your previous language strategy. The more you practise using positive language, the more you will find yourself talking about the flip side – the up side – of an event or happening, and this leads to feeling even more positive about events in the past that already felt good, and feeling much less "down" about events in the past you previously struggled to feel anything but negative about.

## *Refuse to accept the "can't" . . .*

I can't, or I cannot, is one of the most restrictive phrases in the English vocabulary. But, let's cut to the chase – do you continue to do the same thing for the rest of your life, or do you take the action needed today to make the changes and get on with your life?

The changes you are going to make in the future are changes that will be shared with everyone around you and anyone who comes into contact with you. Think back to your legacy statement; what would those closest to you have said about you in the past and now in the present . . . and what are they going to say about you in the future? How has it changed? What would you have honestly said about yourself in the past, and now in the present? How has it changed . . . and how will it change in the future?

The action you take every day is a direct reflection of what you are doing towards achieving your legacy. Keep this in mind and all else will work in your favour, but make sure you update your legacy and your actions accordingly. For example, you may want to be an astronaut when you're 5 years old but that may not be your reality when you're 35 years old! Things change and legacies change, but time spent feeling bad about what may or may not happen in the future is time wasted. Any such negative "what if?" thoughts can only restrict your ability to think and live *in the present* . . . and here, in the present, is where the action is!

Accept that you have no control over the past or the future, only the micro second that you are in now, in the present moment. In my mind, the past is called the past because it is just that – PAST. In the same way that you might pass by a service station on the motorway, it's now behind you and you are unable to turn around to go back. The next service station and your future are now ahead of you and it is one-way traffic.

 **Task**

Start to think about the "right" reasons for change; the positive reasons for change, and list them:

I want to change ......................................... because...........
.............................................................

Do this for each of your issues. A sense of clarity always comes from getting things down on paper.

## Realigning your dreams

It can be very easy to lose sight of what it is you want in life, leading to a tendency to focus on the issues, problems, and things you *don't* want in life instead. However, knowing what you don't want is in fact a fantastic way to start moving forward with your change and to begin improving the quality of your life. What you want and what you don't want aren't necessarily opposites; they are usually very closely linked.

It's all too common in modern day thinking to focus on what we don't want in order to avoid it, but this way of thinking has always baffled me as we tend to go in the direction that we look. There's an expression, "What you think about, you bring about," which backs up my point perfectly. If you focus on what you *don't* want, you bring the things that you don't want into your life. Of course, thinking about something won't make that something materialize in front of you, but by holding negative thoughts in your mind, you generate negative emotions that you carry around with you. For example: you might be thinking, "I don't want to be eaten by a bear." Is being eaten by a bear something that's likely to happen to you? Probably not; but by carrying thoughts of how awful it would be to be eaten by a bear around with you, you are effectively *living* that nightmare scenario!

> "Some of the worst things in my life never even happened"
>
> Mark Twain

By the same token, fearing the unknown is a bit of a cop-out in my world. Being fearful about something that hasn't actually happened doesn't actually make much sense, and with any kind of logic applied, it's really slightly daft!

For example, look at the following statements:

- I am fearful about losing my girlfriend because she may find someone better looking.
- I am fearful about aliens landing because some people say that they have seen them.

Do you see one of the above statements as more plausible than the other? Why is it that? Both could *potentially* happen, yet one seems more unlikely than the other: both could theoretically happen, yet one seems more acceptable than the other. Why? Your mind gauges how realistic something is based on the number of times it has actually happened, or the number of times you *believe* it to have happened. We are constantly bombarded with media images of celebrity couple "break ups" and infidelities so, whether you have any personal experience of heartache or not, you accept it as potential happening based on the frequency of it happening to others. An alien landing, on the other hand, is not so commonly reported and therefore it's an eventuality that's not so readily accepted as likely to happen!

The bottom line is that, if you look hard enough, you are likely to find "reasons" to start believing that something that hasn't happened *will* happen. One of my father's many pearls of wisdom is "Those who look for trouble will always find it." These are wise words and very true because your internal programming in this instance will start to cross-reference information previously learned or seen (although *not* necessarily real) and create behaviours, or notice situations, that represent the something or the situation being a *real* and true happening or a potential happening.

 **Task**

To demonstrate the above point, have fun trying out the following:

Next time you are out with your partner or with friends, play the "how many red cars can you see" game! You can of course substitute "red cars" with anything of your choice, and obviously this is a game you can only play when it's safe to do so (be aware of the potential dangers of **deletion** when driving), but you will be amazed by what you begin to notice when you're looking for something in particular – things your mind previously deleted because they were considered unimportant and not worthy of attention.

My friends have sometimes commented on my tendency to avoid looking at negatives as "odd." My response is always to question and ask: why would anyone look into doing something and then choose to focus on all of the negative reasons, or reasons they wouldn't succeed? That approach seems much more "odd" to me. When setting out on any task, always look for the reasons why you *can* achieve rather than the reasons why you *cannot* achieve. Looking at life in this simplistic way will often bring about its own challenges, but the journey will be a whole lot more enjoyable.

*"If you're not enjoying the journey, you're unlikely to enjoy the destination"*

## Think . . .

Take a moment to think about what you want and the *positives* it would bring into your life. Ask yourself this question:

*If you weren't being you right now, but you were being the person you want to be, what would you be doing?* In fact, **create your own super-ego!** *If you were being the perfect you – the "you" who is able to deal with any situation, any engagement, and any confrontation – how would you look; how would you act?*

Get to grips with who you truly are, and get professional about it. The more you accept and believe that you are worth everything you attract, the more your life will give you exactly what you want. I know because it has happened to me. The more I look back on my life, the more I see all of the aspects I attracted. Everything from my attempted "divorce" to the near collapse of my business was the result of my thinking and my lack of ability to see objectively *in the present*. Every happening in your life, both positive and negative, is a reflection of your thinking.

## *Get proud and loud . . .*

Knowing "who" you are rather than "what" you are is your new mission. Get proud and get loud, not vocally, but in the way that you present yourself physically. Enjoy your newly found confidence and attempt new things that in the past you would never even have contemplated.

Write down two things you have not done in the past because you thought you couldn't; things that effectively represent the complete opposite of what you thought it was possible for you to achieve. For example, if you are fearful of heights this might be a bungee jump, or if you are fearful of public speaking this might be attending a networking event.

Whatever you have written down, **now go and do it!**

Push your opposites and uncover your true potential. Remember, you are more than just your physical body.

## *Be aware of over thinking . . .*

Choose *not* to accept negatives as failures, and adopt an attitude of "there is only feedback" instead. With this mindset in place, you stop the attachment of negative emotions to an event, meaning you are free to learn from the experience and **move on.**

I have retrained my mind to think this way, so that any event that passes can now only be seen as a positive. My attitude is that if you can close your eyes and still *see* a particular event then you are dependent on the feelings associated with what you see. People often refer to feeling numb about a negative event and that's fine, it's in this state of numbness that you can act, utilizing the lack of feeling to move forward with your change. The longer you hold on to feelings of *failure*, the longer you remain stuck there . . . stuck in that place of *failure* and unable to move on.

Modern psychology has always inspired me; especially the way it has evolved and how theories once believed to be true have now been shown to be quite the opposite. Things change because boundaries are constantly being pushed. We learn through feedback; feedback *is* learning, and through feedback we learn and move on.

 **Think . . .**

As if having to deal with a negative event once isn't bad enough, putting yourself back into that emotional environment time and time again is *not* progress. **Visit the situation, learn from it, accept it, and MOVE ON** . . . you wouldn't keep putting your hand on a hot stove just to remind yourself how painful it was the first time, so stop doing it with your past memories!

Replacing "failure" with "feedback" allows you to move forwards. In fact, the act of replacement can be an effective way to change your focus from what you *don't want* onto what you *do want*. There is a common feeling, within the weight-loss industry in particular, that it's all about the taking away! *You can't do this, you can't have that, and don't even think about eating those* . . . but this approach isn't working! Taking away generates negative emotions, but by simply changing your mind-set you can flip the emotions attached to the actions you are taking. For example:

- "I don't want to eat chocolate" focuses your mind on what you don't want and on the *taking away* but,
- "I am really looking forward to having my nut selection" switches the focus to what you *do* want and the positives of the actions you are taking.

When you're thinking badly, you'll be acting badly. Failure is generally considered to be a negative but it's a negative that can be removed by simply changing the word "failure" to "feedback" and therefore "learning" – you can only ever succeed when you're learning! How much more would you do and what new things would you attempt if you could never fail, you could only learn how to do or how not to do something?

There is an inner sense of achievement gained through making change happen, but there's an even greater sense of achievement in creating a strategy you can apply to implement change on any occasion and any time it's needed. The best feeling is the feeling of *knowing* you can . . . with this feeling comes *true* confidence.

Be courageous in your change: there is perhaps no greater sense of achievement to be gained than that of knowing that you can and will stand up against the things that conflict with the *true* you and living a *true* life. Some examples of conflict might be terrorism, murder, rape, theft, etc., but I am not suggesting you become a freedom fighter, mercenary, or even an active campaigner, I'm suggesting that you stand up for what is categorically right and wrong! Be the type of person who fails to turn a blind eye: I would certainly step in if someone was attempting to harm my neighbour, even if stepping in goes against another's better judgement.

I am a fan of police action TV shows, and I remember in one particular show there were two police officers attempting to bring a drug dealer to the ground. It was later revealed by CCTV cameras that members of the public had stood by and recorded the event, even though one of the officers was stabbed in the head with a key during the proceedings. As I watched the show, I remember thinking how obscene it was that 30 or so citizens witnessed the event yet not one stepped in, not even to offer support to the officer after he sustained serious injuries.

Although these happenings are rare, and an eventuality I hope none of us should face, pre thinking about a courageous act brings about an internal confidence that generates the ability to act should a situation arise. It's the *knowing* how to act that supports the good deed. See yourself as the one who would do something where others would turn and look away: be the one who stands up for the law of the land, and be proud of standing for what you know is universally right and wrong. Others will follow, and your external to internal fulfilment will develop; your confidence will grow, and so will your inner smile – all through knowing that you can achieve anything when you are able to see clearly.

## *Make a promise to yourself . . .*

### Do one thing every day that makes the next an exciting new adventure.

If you choose to muddle on through life assuming that things are going to change in the future, even though you're doing nothing about it, you're on a slippery slope. The more you instil these negative affirmations, the more your subconscious uses them as a way to muddle on without recognizing the need to pause and think about the action you are taking and the effect it is having on your life. Instead, choose to take back control of your thinking and spend some time just thinking about the choices you are making in the present. It's important to think *in the present* and not to think ahead to how your actions will affect your life in the future.

A good friend and mentor of mine always starts his seminars by asking people where they are. I love this and always enjoy the variety of responses, everything from naming the exact seat number they are sitting in, to where they are in the world, but very few people actually use the word "present" in their response.

Now for me, the word "present" has a deeper and further meaning; that meaning in a nutshell is simply to be present in that moment and to push it only as far ahead as the next moment, so that you are only ever taking action when you are in that "present" state. With society pushing from all angles and the many stresses of modern life, it's very easy to slip into constantly thinking about "stuff" a few steps ahead – stuff like, "What's for dinner tonight; are the kids at an afterschool club; are my direct debits set up, or is it time for my afternoon break?" It doesn't matter what the stuff is or what it is you're thinking about it, the fact remains that you're spending time thinking about something that isn't ready for that thought.

Yes, we need to plan, but time spent planning and time spent answering the daily questions that come up should be time that's specifically set aside for that purpose. Being present is a strength that very few people can actually master, but it's something that needs to be practised if your change is going to be a permanent process.

So how do you get into the perfect state of being in the present?

First, you have to forgive; resentment, hate, and other negative "cling-ons" can cloud your judgement . . . and the choices you make. Forgiveness and letting go are important elements of rounding the edges of your building blocks, and therefore the whole process of change.

There's a Buddhist parable that beautifully illustrates the importance of letting go. It's known as "The Story of the Two Monks and a Woman" and the following version is from PracticalBuddhist.com:

### The Two Monks and a Woman

Two travelling monks reached a river where they met a young woman.

Wary of the current, she asked if they could carry her across. One of the monks hesitated, but the other quickly picked her up onto his shoulders, transported her across the water, and put her down on the other bank. She thanked him and departed.

As the monks continued on their way, the younger monk was brooding and preoccupied in thought. Unable to hold his silence, he spoke out. "Brother, our spiritual training teaches us to avoid any contact with women, but you picked that one up on your shoulders and carried her!"

"Brother," the second monk replied, "I set her down on the other side, while you are still carrying her."

The second monk's thoughts and actions are a perfect example of being *in the present* and taking responsibility for his own actions. He didn't allow thoughts of past experiences *or* future experiences to cloud his judgement . . . he responded in the *now*, and then let that moment go to be fully present in the next moment. The other monk *didn't* let go; he allowed himself to become weighed down with negative emotions surrounding the happening that was now already in the past. This meant he was unable to move on, effectively stuck on the river bank and unable to be *in the present* in the moments that followed.

 **Task**

The following simple exercise is a great demonstration of how you can, if you choose, bring about instant changes to your body and your mind.

**Change the inner world and the external will change all by itself. It's that simple.**

If you can change the way the world looks then the world will look at you with a completely new set of eyes.

Try it now:

- Wherever you are, take a few moments to think about all of the negative things in your life right now. Let's say no more than 10 seconds: think about debt, family stress . . . you get the idea.
- Pay attention to your body language and the way you say things internally; notice whether you look up or down as you think of negative things . . .
- Now flip it: think about all of the positive things in your life right now – friends and family, the affectionate smile of a loved one, the freedom you have, or the exciting changes that may be about to happen.
- Now notice your body language . . . are you less slumped; are you smiling? If you notice you're still slumped, extend your back and make yourself taller, then add a smile by thinking the best thoughts you are able to produce. If needed, it can be helpful to think about a time when you were feeling your very best and recapture all of the amazing emotions flowing through each of the nerve fibres and cells in your body. Pay attention to the way you feel and notice the increase in energy that comes with it.

Your mind–body connection is more than just your inner thoughts and words; it's the relationship between achieving and not achieving. The way you think is the way you feel – feel good on the inside and that feeling will be radiated on the outside; feel bad on the inside and that feeling will be radiated on the outside.

## *No time like the present . . .*

Look beyond the boundaries held within your mind and keep your mind open to change, but create a practical approach to making your changes. For example, today may not be the best time to take action on your career but next week may be. Only you will know when the time is right but you must set that time in stone and not allow your change to be delayed by a never-ending list of non-existent "reasons" to put it off to another day. "Another day" is code for "never going to happen"!

**Stop thinking that you can't. If you spend just a few moments reflecting on what you achieved as a child – and in a very short period of time – it quickly puts what you *can* do into perspective.**

There are many life situations that can make us feel we have been backed into a corner and the only way out is to adopt our innate "fight or flight" response. However, neither fighting nor taking flight is very productive. Fighting is never a great way to act and running away isn't going to solve anything as the issue will still be there when you come back. The way out is to replace "fight or flight" with "think and respond" instead. "Think and respond" is an approach I chose to adopt after watching my brother-in-law in action as a senior martial arts teacher. Every action he took was calculated and well thought through, and his awareness of the situation in the present allowed him to respond in the best way possible to each situation and in each moment of time. His ability to think and respond was the result of having a clear mind, free of unnecessary "stuff" and clutter, and consequently being able to think and act in a state of being totally present.

**Aspire to be the best you can by doing the best you will.**

Rounding the edges is your way of ensuring you give yourself the best start as you begin to build your temple. You are making the absolute most of the solid foundations you have prepared by clearing everything that's unnecessary and likely to slow your progress out of the way. You are choosing to keep hold of only the things that *really* matter in terms of your lasting legacy, and you're making space for those things by letting everything else go. Overcoming negativity in your past is one thing, but it's essential to take the stance that once you have overcome it, you will not allow your future to become a remake of your past. Learn from your past, then let it go, making a conscious decision never to turn back. Once you have mastered the ability to control your mind and your emotions, you will be able to make clear decisions focused towards achieving a better, more fulfilled and successful life.

## Rounding the edges checklist

- ☐ Identify what *really* matters to you in life
- ☐ Take responsibility for *all* of your thoughts and actions
- ☐ Make choices and *follow* through on those choices
- ☐ Accept that things will not get better unless you **do something**
- ☐ Discard limiting beliefs and negative baggage
- ☐ Choose to think and act **in the present**

# Step Three
# SETTING THE STONE

"You cannot dream yourself into a character; you must hammer and forge yourself one"

*– James A Froude*

So why is it that some people can make changes and some are stuck? Why is it that some people can get on with their life after facing some extreme event and others will stay within the shadows for many years?

These are questions that have inspired me for many years, and they have sent me on a quest to find the answers. Is it possible to control your thoughts and *really* bring about a positive change? Do the people who successfully make changes hold a clue or a secret? No; they simply take the massive action needed to implement the change and they continue along that path.

As an action junkie, I love the gym and I love running; I often take my dogs down to the beach in all weathers to just run . . . Forrest Gump style. The positive feelings generated as a result of this action push me to achieve more on the next run, and then the next . . . just one step at a time.

## One step at a time . . .

When you work on the basis of taking one step at a time, anything is achievable. I promise you this; if you *take* action and you *keep* taking it one step at a time, anything is achievable – no matter how small those action steps are. What you can achieve has nothing to do with your current standing, but everything to do with the one to which you aspire.

A motto I live by is: **"It's not where we start in life, but what we do with life that counts."**

> *"It matters not what someone is born, but what they grow to be"*
>
> J K Rowling

Nothing is unachievable if your mind is given a map. Just as you wouldn't start a journey without knowing the destination, your mind must be given specific tasks that act as map coordinates in order to guide you to the right place. What this means is that getting to where you want to go is based on knowing where you have already been . . . or, if you think of it another way, everything you achieve is a direct result of everything you have already seen. Your journey will take you from "who" you are to "who you are to become" but, as you learned in Step One, it's not about the destination, it's about the journey, so the number of steps you take to cross *your* pond on *your* journey is ultimately *your* choice. Of course, knowing "who" is waiting for you on the other side makes every step you take a whole lot easier, but care must be taken to ensure that every step is a step in the right direction. Before stepping away from a situation that seems unimportant, test the step against your values first.

## Can you really achieve it?

The information we use to gauge our future is based on the environment we are placed in at this very moment . . . and it's more information than you think!

Look around you right now . . .

- How is the environment you're in affecting you?
- What could you do to change the visual aspects of the world around you?
- How would changing the visual aspects change the way you think?
- Would it change the way you think?
- How could you improve the environment you're in?

As any "home makeover" presenter on daytime TV will tell you, changing the environment in your home can be as simple as changing your colour scheme or rearranging your furniture. Whether or not you subscribe to the idea of feng shui, it's fair to say that even small changes in your living environment can lead to big changes in your overall mood, with time spent in the "new" environment giving you an emotional lift.

In Step Two, you learned that by changing your inner world, your external world will change all by itself. *If you can change the way the world looks then the world will look at you with a completely new set of eyes.* Using the above "home makeover" example, there have been occasions when the owner of the home feels so dissatisfied with their environment that they want to sell up and move. It might be that the rooms feel too small, too big, too odd-shaped, too conventional . . . and the list of negatives they see goes on. *Everything* about the environment has become negative because of the way they see it. When the fresh eyes of the makeover team arrive, they, of course, see things quite differently. They see all of the positives in the environment and they make use of those positives to make the best of the rooms. The changes they make are often very small but the outcome of those changes is that the owner sees things differently and therefore feels differently about the environment – they can now see the positives, and they no longer want to sell up and move. Those positives were there all along, but the negative inner environment in the home owner's mind created a negative outer environment in which only negatives could be seen.

## Changing your inner environment . . .

Internal changes lead to external changes and this means it's possible to look in the mirror and see a **new you**. Can you think of a time when you've looked in the mirror and felt really good about what you saw? It may be a time when you were all dressed up for a special occasion and the feel-good emotions could be seen radiating from your face and body. Wouldn't it be good to feel this way *every* time you looked in the mirror? You *can*.

How?

It's very simple: honesty is a key factor when making changes. Simple but effective changes in the way you communicate with yourself about your physical looks can bring about radical changes in your behaviour. Think about this for a moment; if you look in the mirror and send out "fat" or "ugly" signals, then that's exactly what you'll find. To see a new you in the mirror, you need to create a new identity. Your new identity must be the *true* you. If you have yet to discover who you *really* are, refer back to the "True Me" exercise in Step One and identify the *real* you before reading any further. You have to know who you are in order to know who you are to become, and building your temple on the foundations of a false (or mistaken) identity is like building on foundations of sand.

Self-awareness is something that sets humans apart from the majority of other animals. We are able to see and recognize ourselves in a mirror, whereas a dog, for example, sees another dog rather than a reflection of itself. "The Mirror Test" was pioneered by psychologist Gordon Gallup Jr. in 1970 and is now considered the classic test of self-awareness in animals; with a variation of the original format used in developmental psychology to test self-awareness in babies and young children. In the fast moving world of technology, The Mirror Test is now also being used in the development of artificial intelligence, with a robot named Nico set to "pass" the self-awareness test and become the first *thinking* robot. While this may strike fear into the hearts of all those who saw the 2004 movie *I, Robot*, starring Will Smith, it's quite fascinating to think that we're on the threshold of replicating this most human-like *awareness* in the computerized "mind" of a robot.

Of course, we still have so much to learn about the human mind and the inner workings of the brain. Understanding that we have an awareness of "self" is only the tip of the iceberg . . .

- . . . What image of "self" does an anorexic see reflected in the mirror?
- . . . What image of "self" does a narcissist see in the mirror?

Science doesn't have all the answers but, clearly, the image an individual sees of themselves in a mirror is not necessarily the same image another person sees when looking at them in the same mirror. In each set of eyes, the image they see is believed to be a *true* image, demonstrating the power of the mind and its ability to influence the thoughts and behaviours of each individual. If you *believe* something to be true, it *is* true – for *you*.

## Success preparation

To achieve the success you want to achieve, you must *believe* that's it's possible for you to achieve it. You must be able to look in the mirror and see the *true* you; the "success in the making" you, and the "best you" you're on your way to becoming by taking massive action to implement the necessary changes.

*"Success is liking yourself, liking what you do, and liking how you do it"*
Maya Angelou

Think about it this way; are you more likely to achieve something you want by . . .

- Believing it is **possible** – acting and utilizing positive intentions to create paths and strategies with added resourcefulness, and adopting a state of *doing* rather than *being*?
- Or, believing it is **impossible** – acting in a way that's demoralising?

To succeed, you must *prepare* to succeed. This means you must:

- **Believe in yourself** – *you* must believe you can succeed.
- **Value yourself** – you must believe you deserve to succeed.
- **Invest in a good education** – you must invest in learning from the best to become *your* best. However "best" does not always equate to most expensive or most prestigious; the best education is found in learning from masters of the art who pass on their knowledge through loving what they do and doing what they love.

## Repetition provides perfection . . .

Just as a stonemason makes many small alterations to the cornerstone in the process of setting the stone, your persistence with any action will embed this new pattern within your thinking. Consistent actions become actions you are able to do without "thinking" about doing them. When you consistently see the positives in your environment or consistently look in the mirror and see the true you, you reach a level of subconscious competence that makes seeing the world and yourself in this way your default setting: you *learn* to see the *best you* in the mirror without consciously thinking about it, just as a stonemason learns to alter and set the stone as if it were second nature.

## The Four Stages of Learning

"The Four Stages of Learning" is the name given to a theory developed by Noel Burch at Gordon Training International in California in the 1970s. In a nutshell, it's a model for learning that began as a model for learning new skills. The "four stages" map the journey from being unaware of incompetence – not knowing what you don't know – to achieving subconscious competence – able to apply or carry out what you now know without thinking about it.

### Stage 1: Subconscious Incompetence

In this stage, you're unaware of your incompetence so, in other words, you don't know what you don't know. You may be completely unaware or you may believe that the knowledge or skill you don't have is something you don't need; you're unaware of the positive benefits it could bring into your life. It only becomes possible to progress beyond this stage when you recognize for yourself that there's something you don't know and realize the benefits of changing your status through learning.

*"Ignorance more frequently begets confidence than does knowledge"*

Charles Darwin

## Stage 2: Conscious Incompetence

In this stage, you haven't acquired the new knowledge or skill but you recognize the benefits of acquiring it. It's having an understanding of the benefits that not only allows you to begin the learning process, but also to accept the inevitable process of trial and error you're likely to go through on the way to acquiring it.

## Stage 3: Conscious Competence

In this stage, you have gained the new knowledge or learned the new skill but applying or practising it takes concentrated effort; you're effectively still learning and embedding the new pattern or "setting the stone" through careful and deliberate repetition.

## Stage 4: Subconscious Competence

In this stage, the new knowledge or skill can be applied without consciously thinking about it and the learned pattern is now so firmly embedded that it can be demonstrated effortlessly.

Any knowledge or skill you have acquired to the level of subconscious competence is something that feels like second nature to you.

So, to put the above "four stages" into context, let's say you've never learned to drive because you live in an inner city apartment and therefore you've never felt it was a skill that would be of any benefit to you in your life (Stage 1). You then come to the realization that you're longing for a change of pace and change of lifestyle – you want to move out of the city. During the search for your new home, you also come to realize that your options are restricted by your need to have easy access to public transport. The value of learning to drive now becomes apparent to you (Stage 2). You find your dream home in a rural location – several miles away from the nearest town with public transport links – and this galvanizes your decision to learn to drive. You book yourself a course of driving lessons and the learning process begins. At the end of the course, you feel confident enough to book a driving test, which you pass, but you're aware that you've never driven "alone" without supervision (Stage 3). You buy your first car and drive without supervision for the first time, gradually building your skills and your confidence by getting behind the wheel every day. Before you know it, you're driving without consciously thinking about driving – you're effectively driving on "auto pilot" (Stage 4).

Knowledge is power and, in the above scenario, knowledge is also freedom. Learning to drive opened up a whole new world of possibilities in terms of finding a new home and adopting a new lifestyle: learning allowed you to change your life for the better.

**It's never too late to learn: learning is for life, not just for school, but . . .**
**BIG TIP – avoid any kind of learning that restricts the mind.**

Of course, making the decision to learn something new doesn't guarantee you success, instant or otherwise. However, there is never any shame in giving the decision you make your best shot. Things may not turn out exactly as planned, but when you've done your best by committing yourself to a task, you have not shamed yourself or let yourself down . . . and you have not let anyone else down. You see, you cannot let anyone else down before letting yourself down, and when you have done your very best, you have no reason to feel any emotional shame.

## *Learn then lead . . .*

Learn then lead – this was a great saying that I heard back in 1999 when going through my secondary phase of Army basic training. "Cubby," the sergeant at the time, said "In order to lead you must read: learn the topic, create a solid understanding, and then lead by sharing it." You will meet people who lack understanding, and through the use of their strength and "power" will attempt to belittle the "ideas person" who wants to share rather than learn from them. This is common in modern structured cultures and it's an attitude that is very often reflected in the morals of such individuals.

However, this is not the case with the likes of Virgin, Boots, or Apple. In these highly successful organizations, an employee at any level with an idea worth sharing is someone who will be listened to, and the "powers that be" listen *not* because they have to, but because they choose to . . . and they choose to because they are interested.

> *"Having a personality of caring about people is important. You can't be a good leader unless you generally like people. That is how you bring out the best in them"*
> Sir Richard Branson

## *Keep learning . . .*

Study the human response . . . and keep learning. The way that you will act in a situation is largely based on your previous learning; however, by studying the behaviours and actions of others, you can further your own learning by paying attention to how they respond in the same situation . . . or any given situation.

We have no control over the actions of others, but we have absolute control over how we *interpret* those actions. Although I appreciate the advances of modern technology, there are now many more instances of miscommunication; and the further removed from face-to-face interactions we become, the greater the potential for messages to be interpreted incorrectly.

**Think about the following scenario . . .**

You are just about to leave the company where you have worked for over 10 years: you are leaving to have a child and you don't intend to return. Your boss has arranged a party and you are just on your way out when your phone bleeps. The message is from your boss and reads: "Can't make it tonight, good luck."

*What are your first impressions?*
*Would you feel angry; disappointed?*

You go to the party. As you arrive, you are greeted by a fellow colleague who asks, "Have you heard the news?" The news is that your boss has been involved in a car accident and her child has been injured. You immediately feel a sense of guilt and experience emotions of sadness over pre-judging your boss on her brief words.

From this point forward, make the conscious choice to base emotions and behaviours on physical interaction rather than "faceless" technology. If you receive a message via these channels, avoid adding any emotional attachment to the words. As you read on through the contents of this book, you will become increasingly aware of the need to play along with the emotions you experience in life; questioning and judging them to see what will come true. One thing that's for sure is that you need to know *all* the facts before you pass judgement.

## Visualizing a completed you

The external image others see of you is an image you are constantly judged by. However, it's a purely superficial image. The *true* you is the person you are on the inside, so it's only possible to create a true image of you by combining external *and* internal images to reveal the *complete* you . . . the *best* you.

To see the true you, you need to see beyond the reflection in the mirror to the inner you. Visualizing a completed you begins by transforming the way you *think* of yourself. This is not something many get or take the opportunity to do within a lifetime, but you can . . . and you can start right now.

### *Knowing the* true *you* . . .

Knowing who you really are is the foundation on which the process of change is built, but knowing how you came to be the person you are is fundamental to understanding how you can change and why change is needed in your life.

You are who you are based on three important aspects:

**One** – the first person you are is based on the person you were told you were. This person is likely to have been formed during your early childhood, your imprint stage, and is therefore largely a reflection of the environment and behaviours of those around you at that time in your life. This could be considered the past you; but while memories of this period are likely to become blurred and lack any real clarity, emotions are likely to stay strong, and it's from these emotions that the second person is most likely to evolve.

**Two** – the second person is the person you think/believe you are. This is the person you see when you look in the mirror; the person who has evolved from the imprint period in your life. This could be considered the present you, and this person is based on everything you have chosen to accept as real or not real about yourself and your environment along the way.

**Three** – the third person is the person you truly are. This is the person you aspire to become and so could be considered the future you. The harsh reality is that most people will not achieve this person in their lifetime simply because their belief in the second person, the person they *think* they are, restricts their movement towards becoming the person they *truly* are.

Change can take a second to implement and offer a lifetime of rewards: your change starts the second you take the action to do something about it. It's a misconception and a myth that it takes time to see the positive effects of change. A simple change in your diet, for example, can bring about visual and emotional changes within a week, and changes to your outlook on your career can bring about changes within minutes of sitting at your desk. The image of "self" you create is powerful, so a change for the better in terms of learning to think of yourself and see yourself as a success is an essential step towards becoming your best self. Confidence can be found by really getting to grips with the *true* you; and knowing who you really are on the inside makes it possible to begin expressing who you really are on the outside.

**Trust the *true you* by choosing NOW to accept that you deserve more, you deserve better, and you *can* have it.**

 **Task**

To move from being the person you *think* you are to being the person you *truly* are, you need to identify which beliefs you have about the current you that are accurate, honest, and *real*. The simplest and most effective way to do this is to write them down in a notebook in a section dedicated to "Beliefs" – and use the title "The Beliefs I Have About Myself."

You can refer to this page every day or every other day, but refer to it at least once a week for six weeks. Each day you refer to your notes is an evaluation day, a day in which you give yourself the opportunity to question the beliefs you have written down.

For example, your notebook page may look as follows:

07/01/2013
I will never get the job promotion I want because I am not good enough.

08/01/2013
My relationships always fail because I am boring.

11/01/2013

I will never get the grades I need because I am not intelligent enough.

Choose *not* to accept the negative beliefs you have about your current self, choose to question them, and choose to accept the positive beliefs of the true you; the person you aspire to be instead. Remember, knowing who you *really* are provides you with the rock solid foundations on which the process of change can be built. However, beware evaluating your beliefs on a "bad day" – a day when your thoughts and behaviour are somewhat different to your usual state. Any decisions made outside of the *true you* state are unlikely to be productive.

When you are having a "bad" day, it's likely that a number of things will happen. The first is that your body will take on a physical demeanour that shows how "bad" you're feeling; the second is that you will create a number of visual cues that represent a past negative state; and the third is that you will communicate in a way that provides the easiest option under the circumstances as you see them.

## Be aware of stacking . . .

Stacking is a term I've coined to describe the process of adding one issue on top of another until the situation becomes unbearable. When you stack your issues, you are effectively confirming their existence; you are convincing yourself that all of the negatives in your life are real and that you're right to continue with your negative strategies. The more you stack, the heavier the weight of negative emotion you add, so next time you *choose* to have that emotion or practise that strategy the quicker you can adopt that negative state.

It's like stacking your dirty plates in the sink and never washing up. You need to keep eating but eventually you'll run out of clean plates, and your sink will be overflowing!

## Installing a learning mind-set

Learning is easy when you are passionate about the end result, and the same can be said of change. The more excited you are about the benefits of making a change, the easier it is to make that change or, put another way, the bigger the reward the better the journey. Over the years I have always given myself various targets and rewards as incentives, many of which massively outweighed the actual amount of work I needed to put in to merit getting them. My reason for doing so is simple: a big reward encourages a big effort – often encouraging me to over-achieve – and when you're rewarded for achieving one task, you're much more likely to set yourself another one . . . and another . . . The incentives can be hourly, daily, or weekly, and perhaps eventually scaled down to monthly or even yearly, but having those incentives in place and making them visual reminders of what you are working towards can provide on-going motivation to implement the changes you want to make.

I have a belief that the only things we cannot do are the things we choose not to do. This bold statement is one that can be set into the stone of your new thinking patterns.

**The only things I cannot do are the things I don't want to do.**

Your first breakthrough will be your best breakthrough: once you have implemented the techniques set out within the pages of this book, your change will happen and your life will change as a consequence. Changing the way you think of yourself and see yourself will release all of the negative connotations that have restricted your life to this point. Releasing negativity frees you to push the limits of your internal beliefs about what is and is not possible; however, letting go of the past is still very often believed to be difficult and is therefore resisted – why is this? The reason why so many people struggle to let go is that there is a "comforting" sense of familiarity in knowing and relying on everything in the past being true.

But is it?

## It's time to plan for the future and not for the past . . .

It can be all too easy to rely on the past to guide you through the future, but this restrictive trait can bring about endless issues and complications. The actions you are taking today *will* affect your future so thinking about making changes tomorrow or another day must be avoided; the delay caused by putting things off until tomorrow will be reflected in your future.

*"You are today where your thoughts have brought you;*

*you will be tomorrow where your thoughts take you"*
James Allen

So, if your life is a direct result of your past, what were you thinking when you made the decision to create the strategies that have brought about the life you have now?

**Think . . .**

- Think back 5 years . . . what decision did you make then that has affected your life?
- Think back 10 years . . . what decision did you make then that has affected your life?
- Think back to your childhood . . . what decision did you make in your childhood that continues to affect your life today?

For example; did you look in the mirror 5 years ago and decide that you were now "too old" to make the career change you first thought about making 10 years ago? Or, did you take on board the ill-advised "advice" of a schoolteacher in your childhood who told you that your dream of becoming a writer was not for "the likes of you" and you should focus your attention on getting a "proper job"?

Your inner you is the person who talks to you and guides you; the inner you is the subconscious mind and the *true* you, and this is the person you must now listen to. Remember, to prepare for success you must believe in yourself and believe in the value of yourself. The *true* you believes in you and your potential to succeed, therefore the only person standing in the way of your success is the person you currently *think* you are.

## Think . . .

Getting to know the voices inside your head is an essential element of change. By knowing when they are active, you gain an understanding of them and this gives you the power to stop them or **change** them.

Changing voices:

- Think about your happy voice; the voice you use inside your mind when you're happy, confident, and things are going well. Think about the way you communicate with yourself internally when you're happy.
- Now think about your angry voice; the voice you use inside your mind when you're unhappy, frustrated, or things are just not going well in general. Think about the way you communicate with yourself internally when you're upset or angry.
- Being aware of and recognizing the internal voices you use are the first steps towards taking control of them. The next step is to write down the differences you notice between the two (or more than two if you become aware of other internal voices you use under different circumstances). For example: does the speed change? Do you speak faster or slower when you're happy or angry? Does the tone change? Do you speak louder or quieter when you're happy or angry? Does the voice generate differences in your posture? Do you

(*Continued*)

become more animated or more subdued when you're happy or angry?

- Now imagine yourself in a situation that would normally bring your angry (negative) voice into play. For example, let's say you're struggling to change your duvet cover! The frustration of not being able to get the duvet into the corners and then discovering you've put it on inside-out or the wrong way round causes the negative voice in your head to tell you things along the lines of, "You're an idiot; you have this same problem every time but you're totally incapable of working it out; you're hopeless; you couldn't organise a p**s up in a brewery; you just *never* learn . . ." Okay, this may be a slightly over-the-top response to the situation but you get the gist!
- Keep the same situation in mind and **change** the voice by changing the speed, tone, volume, posture, and everything else you noticed when comparing the difference between your angry and happy internal voices. Imagine yourself in the same situation but use your happy (positive) voice. As you do so, notice how the situation changes. The whole experience is changed just by changing your internal voice.

**I will become the person I want to be by making the changes needed to be better.**

Becoming the person you want to be means having the confidence to see yourself as someone who already possesses all of the tools needed to implement change . . . and that confidence comes from getting to grips with the true you.

"**Confine-dence**" is my interpretation of **confidence,** meaning simply that the confinement of emotions in any animal for any length of time leads to the suppression of identity; and when someone's identity is suppressed, they become unable to express a true representation of themselves.

It can be useful to design your own inner pathway to the true you, so that you can follow it in your mind using visualization techniques to generate your true state, and create a repeatable positive strategy to keep you moving forwards.

 **Task**

*"Don't just think it, ink it"*

There is nothing more rewarding than getting your thoughts down on paper. You can carry a small notebook around with you or you can use your mobile device, but either way it provides you with the opportunity to make a note of your thoughts as and when they come into your mind. Having this type of written reference can be an extremely useful visualization aid, providing you with motivational prompts that can add depth and texture to the images of what it is you want to achieve.

An example format for your inner pathway might be as follows:

- **Thoughts** – what is the thought; what is the positive thought you want to capture?

*(Continued)*

- **Emotions** – how does it feel when you have this thought?
- **Actions** – what actions would I have to take to make it happen?
- **Promotions** – where/how would the results be shown?
- **Legacy** – when will the legacy come to fruition?

It's important to accept that your world is constantly looking to give you opportunities; opportunities that will make your life happier and healthier in all aspects. The things you need are usually staring you directly in the face, and it's just a matter of reaching out and asking for them.

You have to be really clear on what it is you want to achieve, clarity is king . . .

 **Task**

- Write down just five things that you would like.
- Now write down how you can get those things: ask yourself *"How can I get them?"* and create a step-by-step action plan based on your answers. Depending on what it is you've written down, this may seem like a daunting prospect, but just allocate yourself five minutes to do some research and you may be surprised by your findings.
- Now put your plan into action.

## Moving forward and accepting change

The beliefs you have about yourself and your ability to achieve determine the path you will follow. Beliefs can bring about a sense of clarity in many situations – whether you believe you can or you can't complete a certain task, for example, or whether you believe you can or can't make the changes you desire to bring about your perfect lifestyle. But are those beliefs true? There's a well-known Henry Ford quote that backs up my belief that whatever you *believe* to be true *is* true, for you. "*Whether you think you can or think you can't, you're right.*"

Think about it for a moment: have you ever been involved in an argument or debate where you were so absolutely certain that what you were saying was true that you'd have been willing to bet your life on it . . . only to be *proved* wrong?

- Our ancient ancestors believed that it was worshipping the Sun at the end of each day that guaranteed its return the following day.
- Our not-so-ancient ancestors believed the Earth was flat.
- And in 2012, a number of people believed the world would end on December 21.

Your beliefs, unless controlled and understood, can create havoc if they are not aligned correctly with your life or your strategies.

Some of my clients have suffered some horrific behavioural outcomes through various forms of phobias – *have* being in the past context. Common phobias include claustrophobia, agoraphobia, and a fear of heights, spiders, or public speaking. In its literal sense, a phobia is a fear and whether or not you believe yourself to have a *phobia*, you will have experienced fear: we all know what fear feels like.

Fear in this sense is a negative emotion and, remember, it's only by releasing negativity that you become able to push the limits of your internal beliefs. For as long as you hold on to your fear – irrespective of how rational or irrational it may be – you hold on to the limits it places on your life. For example, if you believe you have a fear of speaking in public, you will avoid any situation that might require you to do just that. Adopting this tactic may not have inconvenienced your life too much up until this point, but then one day you get a golden opportunity to go for a promotion at your work; a promotion that would lead to having your dream job. As part of the interview process, you must give a short presentation in front of a panel of senior executives . . . now what? Holding on to your fear *will* now inconvenience your life; holding on to it will prevent you from achieving something you want to achieve; holding on to your belief that you fear public speaking will keep you stuck where you are – stuck as the person you *think* you are, unable to move on to become the person you *truly* are . . . unless you take massive action to implement **change**.

**You can dwell on the past and create an emotional state that reflects that or you can choose to change and move forwards with an attitude of "I deserve to move forwards."**

## Get scared . . . !

Remember, it's only by mastering the ability to control your mind and emotions that you become able to make clear decisions focused on achieving a better, more fulfilled and successful life. Most of us grow up *fearing* fear – we are effectively taught that fear is a weakness – but fear should be looked upon as a fantastic motivator: fear should be used as a booster to the massive action you are about to take to move your life forward. This means in the above scenario, rather than fearing the prospect of speaking in public, you should turn it around to fear of the outcome of *not* speaking in public!

Get scared about what will happen if you fail to take the action needed to accomplish your task; get scared about living your life in the past; get scared about reaching retirement age only to look back and see a wasted life; get scared about not leaving a legacy, and becoming a distant memory, forgotten within two generations.

Use fear as a motivator to change, and remember, the stronger your motivator – or incentive – the more likely you are to excel at the task in hand.

*"It may be hard for an egg to turn into a bird: it would be a jolly sight harder for it to learn to fly while remaining an egg. We are like an egg at present. And you cannot go on indefinitely being just an ordinary egg. We must be hatched or go bad"*

C S Lewis

Of course, there is never any shame in recognizing that a situation is out of your control and asking for help. There have been many times in my life that the next stepping stone on my journey across the pond was just too far to leap without getting my feet wet; so I asked for help. Asking for help should never be feared, after all, to become the best we must learn from the best, and investing in a good education is a key element of preparing to succeed.

## Are your fears worth listening to . . . ?

Our fears are just like stories; they have a beginning, a middle, and an end. Sometimes our fears *can* predict the future and come true; however, you have to ask yourself: are your stories and fears worth listening to? And is it time to stop listening to the wrong story?

There are many stories of people losing everything before turning things around to build an empire; there are many bible stories and ancient fables that tell of people clearing thorn-torn farms to produce successful crops and other such turns of fortune. In each of these stories *and* your own, the principle is the same: the past must be stripped away to make way for the future or, put another way, the foundation must always be clear before the building can take place.

> *"Our dilemma is that we hate change and love it at the same time;*
>
> *what we really want is for things to remain the same but get better"*
>
> Sydney J Harris

Isn't it time to give up being the person you have become and to take the next step towards becoming the person you want to be; the *true* you? Start to use the words **"What next?"** in your everyday language. These are words that gear up your mind to keep moving forwards, and without a willingness to continue looking for the next step on your journey, opportunities will continue to pass you by.

## Craft your own destiny . . .

If you were to theme your life so far into a story, how would it be told? Would it be a story of an average, fairly normal life? **Stop! Stop pretending your life is normal . . . because it isn't.** Normality doesn't exist, and life is full of dysfunctional people. We are taught that normality is something we should all strive to have in life but, as I see it, the word *normality* could easily be replaced with the word *conformity*. If you choose to conform to the rules set out within "normal" society then you will achieve a normal standard of living and, who knows, you might be able to look back with a sense of accomplishment. But, if you look at the back-story of any individual who has truly achieved in life, you find a story that's far from standard or normal.

Choose *not* to conform. Delete the words "I wish" from your everyday language and replace them with "I will." This is a simple change but a significant one: it's a small step that can make the difference between *actually* achieving and carrying on through life with the *intention* of achieving. Think about it; throwing endless amounts of money into a wishing well is not going to bring about the results you want, but stepping away and investing that money in what you need to *do* next *will* take you a step closer to what you want. The more you put yourself into situations that will bring about the life you want, the more chance you have of achieving the life you want. One thing is for certain; you will never win the lottery if you never purchase a ticket!

It doesn't matter where you're starting from or how much money you have. In fact, it has always been my opinion that money (pure cash) only magnifies the state you are in when you receive it. This is something that is demonstrated time and again through the stories of many lottery winners. People mistakenly believe that life will instantly change for the better through becoming "rich" and that money is the answer to all of their problems. However, money cannot change "who" you are, it can only change "what" you are.

 **Think . . .**

- Take a moment to think about your "happy" self and the person you are when you're happy with life and things are going your way.
- Now imagine that "self" magnified by a multiple of ten. How would you look; how would you sound, and how would you act?
- Take a moment now to think about your "unhappy" self and the person you are when you're unhappy with life and things are not going your way.
- Now imagine that "self" magnified by a multiple of ten. How would you look; how would you sound, and how would you act?

Remember, true wealth is found in your inner smile. If you were experiencing depression, sadness, or any other mental illness prior to having financial abundance, then your state will only be magnified by the amount you receive. This highlights the importance of setting solid foundations on which to build your legacy; setting solid foundations based on what *really* matters to you in life. Building your legacy one stone at a time and setting each stone as you lay it ensures each step in the process is a *lasting* step, and the things that really matter to you in your legacy cannot be moved by any external pressures you encounter on your journey to completion.

Remember, there is no such thing as a quick fix. Building your house on foundations of sand may be quick, but it's not going to be lasting. Avoid looking for, and taking, shortcuts on your journey. It can be all too easy to slip into skipping over behind-the-scenes elements of the building process . . . bodging jobs that won't be seen, or leaving edges unfinished in out of the way places . . . but your mind will never actually be at rest; you will never feel a sense of complete fulfilment or contentment until the whole task is completed, and completed to the best of your ability.

## Do you know what you're really capable of. . . ?

Before leaving this Step, I want to give you some food for thought. In the world of psychological research, opinion is divided over what has the biggest influence on our individual behaviours in life. In one camp, psychologists believe that it's our character or personality that drives our behaviour; but in another camp, psychologists believe that our environment or circumstances are in the driving seat with character and personality very much in the back seat.

## The milgram experiment

In 1963, psychologist, Stanley Milgram, carried out an experiment designed to test obedience to authority. It's now known as "The Milgram Experiment" and to this day remains controversial. Milgram, a psychologist at Yale University, devised the experiment after the majority of accused individuals in the World War II Nuremburg War Crimes Trials used "obedience" to superiors and "just following orders" in their defence. He wanted to know how influential "authority" really was in terms of how ordinary people responded to "orders" that would lead to them knowingly harming another human being.

In a nutshell, the participants in the experiment were all men aged between 20 and 50 years old, and they all volunteered to take part after replying to a newspaper ad requesting volunteers for a "learning" experiment at Yale University. Each participant was paired with another man (who was actually an associate of Milgram's and essentially an "actor") and straws were drawn to decide who would be the "learner" in the experiment and who would be the "teacher" – but this was always fixed so that the genuine participant would play the role of teacher. The learner had a list of word pairs to remember and he was then taken into another room (within earshot) where he was strapped into a chair and connected to electrodes. The teacher's role was to ask the learner to provide the matching pair word to the word he gave, and if the wrong answer was given, he had to give the learner an electric shock. The teacher had a "shock generator" in front of him which had 30 switches, enabling him (or so he thought) to give a range of shocks from very mild at 15 volts all the way to very severe (potentially deadly) at 450 volts.

Of course, the learner deliberately gave wrong answers on most occasions and the teacher had to administer an electric "shock" – the effects of which could be heard! In the same room as the teacher, and sitting close by, there was an official "experimenter" dressed in a white lab coat. Unknown to the participant, the experimenter was also one of Milgrim's associates. The participant was instructed to increase the voltage of the "shock" each time an incorrect answer was given, and on many occasions this led to the participant refusing to give yet another shock. On asking for guidance from the experimenter, they were given four predetermined instructions. The first was, "Please continue." If the participant still refused, the second instruction was, "The experiment requires you to continue." If they still hesitated, the third instruction was, "It is absolutely essential that you continue," and the fourth and final instruction was, "You have no other choice but to continue."

An astonishing 65 per cent of the participants continued to administer "shocks" all the way up to the full 450 volt shock, and *all* of them continued to administer "shocks" up to a voltage of 300 before refusing to give any more. This "willingness" to follow the instructions of an "authority figure," even though they believed that they could hear another human being *screaming* and pleading to be released, is food for thought indeed!

By today's standards, the Milgram Experiment is flawed on many levels, but the results certainly add weight to the argument that *circumstances* drive our behaviour more than *personality* alone. The participants were ordinary men from all walks of life with no history of violence or anything other than normal, decent behaviour . . . yet they were all willing to *knowingly* harm another human being; 65 per cent of them believing they were causing potentially life-threatening harm!

So, how well do you know yourself; how reliable is your character; and do you know what you're capable of under *any* circumstances? Look at it this way; have you ever found yourself acting out of character or doing something against your better judgement because you were "going along" with a crowd?

 **Think . . .**

Look again at your legacy statement: look again at your description of the *true you*.

Ask yourself; how do you want to be remembered after you're gone? What lasting legacy do you want to leave behind?

## Setting the stone checklist

- ☐ Commit to taking **one focused step at a time,** there are no shortcuts to any place worth going!
- ☐ Choose to **change your inner environment** in order to change your outer environment
- ☐ Choose to prepare for success by **believing** in your success
- ☐ Commit to life-long learning; **read then lead**
- ☐ Accept that the only things you cannot do are the things you do not want to do
- ☐ Choose to have confidence in and trust the *true you*

# Step Four
# LEAVING A LEGACY

"I had an inheritance from my father,

It was the moon and the sun.

And though I roam all over the world,

The spending of it's never done"

*Ernest Hemingway,* For Whom the Bell Tolls *(1940)*

Step Four

# LEAVING A LEGACY

I remember once, a few years ago, attending some form of training course and sitting there thinking to myself, "there has to be more to this (life) than learning, teaching, treating . . . then retiring." The focus of the training session was to explain and demonstrate a quick fix solution to money worries that would result in all of us becoming millionaires within a year. As I listened, I started to question my own path: not the journey I had been on to reach this point, or the path immediately in from of me from this point forward, but the path I would leave behind after leaving this body . . . the legacy.

I had discussed death and the afterlife before but I'd never given much thought to the afterlife left within this life! As I began to think about this during the training session, I slowly drifted off into a dazed state – while sitting on possibly the most uncomfortable chair known to mankind – and my thoughts led to a number of questions. The first was: what is more important, the work in this life or the continued work in the next? Would it be possible to create something, not knowing what it was at the time, that would continue to help others when I was no longer in a position to? The second was: is it possible to create something that could be mass produced – thereby helping the masses – that would need little or no physical interaction from me? As my mind drifted further away from the present, I started to think about what would be said at my funeral . . . would anyone turn up, and what would be inscribed on my headstone?

**Beware of the man who seeks greatness as he will do anything in order to achieve it!**

The above pearl of wisdom is another that came from my father. He had a successful football career, but he once told me about the many people around him at the time who paid a heavy price for the same success. This is something that has been echoed recently in the world of cycling, with the realization that Lance Armstrong lost his grip on reality and *literally* did anything and everything he could to get to the top; achieving "greatness" in his view. Both my father and my uncle played professional football and, as part of a football legacy, I have seen first-hand those peers who were unable to deal with the fame . . . and then the rapid transition to *non*-fame. I can understand how hard this must be; one minute being in the public eye and becoming accustomed to being "the face" of the industry, and then the next, all of it being stripped from you as you are effectively thrown away. This simply highlights the importance of **legacy** over any short-term fulfilment. As I have said all along . . .

It's not the end that is important, but the path you
take to get there: the journey to internal fulfilment, and the
legacy you leave.

I'm certain that having read this far, you're already thinking about going out and achieving more, but, before you do, continue to read the final section of this book and use the tools you find within it to help you *really* establish the legacy you are leaving behind.

## Building your temple

My attitude has always been that the Western view on life is incorrect. That view is as follows:

- **Education** – from age 4 years to 16/24 years
- **Employment** – from age 18 years to 75 years
- **Retirement** – from age 75 years to death, which in England and Wales in 2010 was most common at 85 years for men and 89 years for women

This means that, if we average out the above statistics, we are in education for 16 years of our life, in employment for 57 years, and in retirement for 15 years. I looked at these statistics when I was still in my early 20s and made the decision then and there to do something about it: I made the *choice* not to comply.

- Does it make sense to work for a longer period of time than you have in retirement?
- Does it make sense to work for a longer period of time than you have to enjoy the freedom of not being tied to a desk or to a set working hour?

It may not make sense but it's a route through life many people follow because they believe they have no choice and there is no alternative.

Below is the alternative view I chose:

- **Education** – life
- **Employment** – life
- **Retirement** – life

Sometimes I sit on the tube in London and watch people coming and going: they all look the same and they all act the same. It makes me wonder if this is where the term "join the rat race" began! But it doesn't have to be this way. Someone who shares my attitude and demonstrates the benefits of adopting an alternative view of life is Sir Richard Branson. I am a great fan of his, not only because he is massively successful, but also because his chosen "lifestyle" incorporates all three aspects of life – education, employment, and retirement. There can be no denying that Richard Branson is building a lasting legacy; his temple stands on solid foundations, but you don't need to become an entrepreneurial multimillionaire to achieve success . . . your success is your choice.

The temple you are building is *your* legacy, no one else's, and while it can be inspirational to learn from the successes of others, it's important to forge and maintain your own *true* identity.

It took me a long time to realize that not everyone wants to be successful; or to have a large house; or to raise a family;

or to achieve the utmost pinnacle of fulfilment in their life! I couldn't quite understand why anyone would choose this *unambitious* attitude to life: why wouldn't everyone want more; why wouldn't someone want to achieve the best in life? And wouldn't everyone rather enjoy life than struggle along every day? My understanding changed the day I met a lovely, larger than life man in his 50s who owned nothing more than a bicycle, the clothes on his back, a toothbrush and a passport. We were complete strangers but we got chatting over a cup of coffee. During the course of the conversation, stories emerged about his life . . . where he had been and what he had been doing for the last 30 years . . . and then out of the blue he asked me: "How do you cope with all that baggage?" The baggage he was referring to was my ambition and he asked: "What if what you're searching for doesn't produce the results you want and life becomes a struggle for no pay off: wouldn't it be better to live every day as it comes?"

As I look at my life now, it's not about the possessions I have or the successes I have achieved; it's about the enjoyment of the journey and the building of a legacy that can go on beyond my living days. Of course, earning a living and enjoying life's luxuries isn't something I resent being able to do, but it's being able to enjoy each day knowing that tomorrow is going to be an equally good day that makes being where I am not such a bad place to be. This is especially poignant for me, as there was a time on my journey, not so very long ago, when I took knockback after knockback and really began to question whether my chosen path would lead to the outcomes I wanted in life. There can be no doubt that the continual knockbacks led to everyone around me also questioning my path, and this generated an atmosphere of doubt. However, I chose *not* to doubt myself and my resilience allowed me to continue building my temple, one step at a time, on solid foundations.

## Persistence, patience, practice . . . the perfect formula

At one stage on my journey, I left the Army and found myself "unemployable"; so when I say I know how it feels to have nothing, I mean it . . . I was on the bread line for real, and it's not something I say for effect! The point I want to make is that along with change in your life there is inevitably also going to be some form of setback . . . and it's most likely going to hurt. The *true strength* and the building of truly rock solid foundations comes from being able to get back up and continue, knowing that what you're doing is congruent with *your* chosen legacy. History is littered with stories of people who against all odds picked themselves up after facing a setback and carried on to produce a true masterpiece. I would love to know what the geniuses of our time actually said to themselves on those occasions when things didn't quite work out as planned, yet they chose to carry on and give it another go.

> *"I have not failed. I've just found 10 000 ways that won't work"*
>
> Thomas A Edison

In my mind it's simple – **just get over it and get on with making it better.** An Army Sergeant of mine once said to me,

"If it can't make you pregnant then it's not worth worrying about." While this may seem to be a fairly antiquated turn of phrase, there's a "rustic" wisdom in his words and I understand what he means by them. There is nothing to be gained from worrying about things that really are not that big a deal in the grand scale of things – let them go. And, by the same token, when something is not working, there's absolutely no point in carrying on with the same approach, effectively trying to get a square peg to fit into a round hole; it's time to try a different approach.

**It's not rocket science: if it's not working, then work at something that will!**

Sure, we would all love to succeed in everything we do and to finish everything we start but, as the geniuses of our time show us, finishing what you start is only possible when you have the ability to keep going on your chosen path even when faced with obstacles and setbacks.

*"Insanity is doing the same thing over and over again and expecting different results"*
Albert Einstein

To me, failure isn't about the outcome; it's about the emotional feelings attached to failing to complete the task. It's not getting an end result that's different to the planned end result that creates feelings of failure; it's not getting an end result at all through not getting to the end of the task that creates those feelings. For this reason, my tip to you is to only start things you are truly prepared to finish, and commit to seeing through what you begin to the end. However, things change, and whatever it is you commit to seeing through must always be in line with your legacy. If your legacy changes, you must change the path you're on accordingly. The journey you take must always be a true reflection of the lasting legacy you want to leave behind. When you set out with positive intent and the congruity to finish what you've started, I don't believe you can ever really fail. Whether it's your chosen path to work on the shop floor providing an essential service to the public, or to manage the shop floor workers, or to own the shop floor and the whole company, makes no difference. It's doing what you love that matters and when you're doing that, you're on the perfect path for you.

When I was about 5 years old, my father told me that I had a choice; a choice that would shape my life beyond any other choice I would make in life, and it was a choice that would have to be made now. This choice, once made, would be a choice that I'd struggle to change in the future, as to bring about change would involve breaking *habits* established from this point forwards; habits of a "lifetime" that would keep pulling me back to my old ways . . . to the choice I was to make *now*.

Of course, as a 5 year old, I remember thinking my father was simply launching into another one of his long and not-so-interesting stories, but what he said that day would go on to shape my life and also the lives of those closest to me. This is what he said . . .

> Life has two paths, that of the cups and saucers and that of the rollercoaster.

The cups and saucers represent safety and security, they attract the type of person that enjoys knowing where they have come from and knowing where they will go; they spin in the same direction and offer a very limited change in the scenery. It will come and go and each day will seem like the next.

The rollercoaster attracts another type of person. They live with the possibility that life will have its highs but will also have its lows, and although the path is still predestined, the journey is a whole lot more exciting.

Neither one is better than the other, but one will bring about adventure and excitement while the other will bring about stability which, at times, the other will lack.

I made my choice; and in my world, the only life worth living is the life that offers excitement, love, happiness, and challenges. Sure, the actions you take now may be different to the actions you take in the future – you *will* make mistakes, but GET OVER IT! Life will always test your beliefs and your path and, very often, just as you think things are going your way, it will put obstacles directly in your path. That's life.

I asked my wife today; what have you regretted? This was her genuine response . . .

Everything I do is a stepping stone and happens for a reason, and every mistake I make is a lesson to be learned, not a regret to be had.

This was a much better response than I had expected but, in a nutshell, it's spot on! Life is too short *not* to make changes: the sooner you start, the easier it will become.

## *Do it* your *way* . . .

We can all learn from the experiences of others and we can all learn through modelling others. One of my mantras has always been a variation of the popular motivational slogan (and often product promoting slogan!) *"If I can do it, so can you."* My version is; *if someone else has done it and documented their journey, then I can follow the same map.* Modelling a successful individual is *not* attempting to become a carbon copy of that individual, it's about studying the character traits that led to their success and then adopting the same successful thought patterns and consequent actions into your own life and your own chosen legacy. Remember, the temple you are building is *your* legacy, and no one else's.

 **Task**

- Write down the names of some people you admire. They can be people you know personally, or famous people you know of but have never met. They can be people who are alive today, or historical figures from the past. In fact, they could even be fictional characters you've come to know so well they've become "real" – James Bond or Harry Potter for example!
- Next to each name, make a note of the qualities they have that you admire; qualities you would like to adopt.
- Take each quality one at a time and write down the ways in which adopting that quality would have a positive effect on *your* life. For example, you may admire

Richard Branson's adventurous "nothing ventured, nothing gained" spirit. In his legacy, he is using it to break records and set new records, but you don't need to be planning passenger flights into space to benefit from adopting the same spirit. What would it mean to you in terms of *your* legacy?

## Getting on with it . . .

Okay, getting over it and getting on with it may well be easier to say than to do, but one thing that's for certain is that each and every one of us on the Earth's surface will at some point reflect on our day and think of something we wish we could change or do differently. It's inevitable; it's just part of being human and it's the way it has been since the beginning of mankind.

Getting on with it becomes much easier when you can begin each new day with thoughts of what can be achieved, not thoughts of what you did *not* achieve the previous day. When faced with setbacks, it's all too easy to feel overwhelmed by the enormity of the task ahead and to think of giving up rather than seeing it through to the end. However, when you think about it for a moment, a bricklayer could very easily feel overwhelmed by the sheer scale of a project as he looks at the plans: the realization that several million bricks will need to be laid to complete the project could very easily make laying the first brick a daunting task. This takes us full circle back to something you learned in Step One . . .

The most common reason why many people fail to change is that they fail to lay their first brick: they stop, often with brick in hand. You only need one brick to start building, but building can only begin when you lay it.

Yes, tasks can seem daunting when you look at the bigger picture but, just as a bricklayer continues to lay one brick at a time to turn plans on paper into a reality, you must take one step at a time to turn your plans for change into your reality . . . to build your temple and make your change a lasting legacy. The bigger picture is made up of many smaller pictures, and it's the culmination of many small projects on a building site that leads to the creation of the final structure. When a structure seems too big to deal with, it can stop you in your tracks with your brick in your hand, but by breaking it down into smaller projects and dealing with each one individually . . . and dealing with it in the present by *not* thinking of the whole structure . . . it becomes possible to *get on with it* and see the building of your temple through to the end from the first brick to the last.

Each and every one of us can apply this step-by-step approach to achieving whatever it is we want in life, yet so many of us continually fail to complete the tasks we set for ourselves: why is this? In my London practice, I deal with all types of clients with all kinds of issues but, before they even arrive, there's one common trait I can practically guarantee will present itself in each of them. I call it the **pre-perception post therapy prediction**: in other words, the thoughts of "I've failed already" that they carry with them as they walk through the door. This trait is commonly found in those looking to lose weight. Most, if not all, of those currently "trying" to lose weight as they walk through the door would have tried at least one diet before, and the previous failure (assuming it failed, hence the reason to attempt an alternative) had already created the presupposition that they were going to fail again. With this in mind, continuing to go through the motions in some way or other acts as an internal buffer; it becomes a subconscious exercise that tricks the conscious mind into producing thoughts and affirmations such as "At least I am trying," or "I am doing my best," or "This isn't working for me." However, the therapy yo-yo effect this creates then becomes a key trigger for the establishment of self-doubt and negative belief patterns. Remember, the building of your temple can only begin once you've prepared the ground . . . and this means clearing away unnecessary baggage.

## Who are you kidding?

Are you "trying"? Are you "doing your best"? Or are you just kidding yourself? This type of internal trickery does not work. The faster you make the choice to change, the quicker that change will happen.

It's up to *you* to take control of your self-image. A lot of the clients that I meet talk about their emotions or feelings as if they are real: making them real makes them appear as something they have, something they are in possession of, and therefore something that can be removed or taken away . . . they will talk about the issue as if it has been given to them as a gift. When dissecting the boastful type of language used, it becomes apparent that there is a sense of normality in having this behavioural defect . . .

- " . . . Oh, I have a phobia."
- " . . . I am scared of needles."
- " . . . I cannot lose the weight."

**If you weren't born with it you don't have to accept it.**

Unfortunately, I lack sympathy with people who aren't willing to let go, and the use of the above language is a common trait among those who are choosing to hold on to the something they *have*. People often come to see me after consulting with another therapist, and my first question is – "why did you decide not to change before?" This confuses almost everyone! But, my reason for asking is to highlight the fact they are looking to the therapist to take away their particular trait/behaviour or strategies, when really the only person who can do that is them.

During speaking engagements, I often refer to a state, belief, phobia, fear, or mental illness as simple labels we use to identify various strategies. As I see it, people who "have" these issues need to understand that they are the ones "doing" the associated behaviours. This is a controversial and often criticized approach, but "having" something leads to the holder looking for someone else to take it from them, whereas "doing" something drives home the point that it's up to them to *stop doing* it! Be aware of using the word "I" in reference to negative issues, as it adds a sense of ownership over those particular strategies. Learn to accept that *everyone* has something they would love to change and you are no different. Accepting that you are not alone can bring about a great feeling of normality, but, avoid being normal . . . as you know already, I am not a great fan of normal! Normal for me is something that takes little effort and demonstrates low standards. **Different is where success can be found.** Our Western culture has set standards in terms of the way we should act or dress, and even the thoughts we should be having, but to make a life of internal success and fulfilment, to make a life that generates an inner smile, you have to go beyond normal.

## *Stop lying and get honest . . .*

The smallest of lies can turn into a big, lifetime obstacle. The more you lie to yourself, and others, the more you tie yourself up in a tangled web that's hard to escape.

> *"Oh what a tangled web we weave when first we practice to deceive"*
> Sir Walter Scott

If you satisfy your thoughts with lies, then your mind, over time, will no longer know what is real and what has been created. This buffer is not conducive to positive thinking. So why do people lie? Lying is a strategy that helps to process a sense of normality, but, let me say it once more – *normality* should not be a target for you! Whenever I hear the word lie, it reminds me of a school playground; children are masters at being able to convince themselves that something is real; they can create and live in fantasy worlds at the drop of a hat; and they can also look you in the eye and tell you that they did not eat the entire packet of biscuits . . . it was the dinosaur sitting opposite them who did that!

## Living with a smile

It's fair to say that living a great life is what most people aim to achieve, however very few actually achieve it. My theory is that if we were to push the boundaries of our lives just a little further, we would more than likely be very happy with the results. For example, let's say your aim is to be able to measure your success on a financial scale, and you set yourself a target of achieving an annual salary of £100 000 in a successful career. If we then assume that you achieve 80 per cent of your target salary, your actual earnings would be reduced by £20 000 per annum. This means that to achieve what you *really* want you must learn to trick your mind with what it is you want *plus* 20 per cent. The tools set out within the pages of this book are designed to help you do exactly that, and the sooner you put them to good use in practice, the sooner you will achieve what you want *and* gain maximum satisfaction from every outcome in life. Do not lie . . . be honest with yourself about what you want, set your ambition scale to full speed, and then push the boundaries just a little bit further; make things just that little bit harder. Your comfort zone, in my opinion, is a place where you have reached your *minimum* standards in life, and by choosing to stay there you have chosen not to grow. In fact, comfort zones don't stay "comfortable" in the long term; they develop into dull, unexciting places in which everything begins to wilt and die. Our emotions are our triggers to happiness and the lack of "fresh air" or movement within a comfort zone allows boredom to arise. My father always used to say, "Boring people get bored," and I use his saying now because it is true in so many different ways. When you stop growing, you stagnate, and the outcome becomes boredom: boredom because you know what you have done and you know what you have to do; boredom because there is limited variation; and boredom because it's unlikely there is ever going to be any variation in the "routine" that has become a life.

## *Start to think differently . . .*

Start to think differently in all areas of your life and in every aspect. Choose to create an inner smile through achieving a life of excellence; a new life that you can look back on during your last days and smile about, knowing you achieved everything within your capabilities and you enjoyed a life of fulfilment as a result.

The key to change is finding the motivation to change. Prioritize your life into distinct areas you want to change – for example, finances, relationships, health, etc. – and think in terms of what you want to change first and last. This doesn't have to follow any particular order but it's important to consider the order in which change is likely to flow. Just as a river flows along the path of least resistance, your flow – your journey – should follow the path where you are least likely to come up against resistance or obstacles that might stop you in your tracks. Remember, the building of your legacy can only begin with the laying of the first brick, so make the first brick something you feel *motivated* to lay in place. With the laying of the first brick, the building of your temple begins. Each new brick laid represents another step and another achievement, and the more you achieve, the greater the advances in terms of the legacy you will leave. However, keep in mind that things don't always go to plan on a building site . . . be flexible! Be flexible with your choices; be flexible in each step you take, and be flexible in the questions you ask yourself and the language you use to motivate change. For example, when things are not going entirely to plan, change negative thoughts of "I can't do this" to positive, productive thoughts of "How can I do this?" Push your boundaries just that little bit further by changing the internal language you use. Eliminating negative words such as can't, won't, and shouldn't will bring with it a completely different strategy that your mind will follow. Negative thoughts and words can only ever bring about a negative outcome; ask for a negative and that's exactly what you'll get, but ask for a positive and that's exactly what you'll get too! It's having this understanding of the link between your thoughts and your behaviours that begs the question – if your thoughts are to become your reality, wouldn't it be wise to create better thoughts?

## Change is as difficult as you want to make it . . .

You can change as fast or as slow as you wish; you can take action or not, but whatever you choose will be the right choice . . . all you need to do is *not* regret it. Regret when you reach a certain age turns into resentment. The more you fail to follow through with your dreams the more your resentment will grow. It's important to accept that life can change in an instant but, when you remain in your flexible state, you can make adjustments to flow with those changes. Life is unfair, get over it! If you are now in your 30s, you are never again going to be in your 20s – let it go! When you hold on to the past, you live in a reactive state but, when you ensure your thoughts and actions are in the present moment, you live in a productive state that will allow you to move on and bring new things into your life.

> "Life is not fair. The only fair you'll get from me is your bus fare home"
>
> Lord Sugar, *The Apprentice*

Think of it this way; do you want to be in your 80s looking back on the exciting achievements of your life and looking forward to leaving a lasting legacy, or do you want to be in your 80s visiting plastic surgeon after plastic surgeon in an attempt to hold on to the youthful looks of your 30s? There comes a point in your life when the character can no longer support the act: a supermodel cannot hold on to her looks indefinitely as she ages, and an Olympic athlete cannot continue to go on improving his performance into his 90s. Choose to make changes that offer longevity, and choose to live for the here and now. Remember, New Year's resolutions fail because they offer no longevity so choose to make a lifestyle change rather than a target driven change.

It can be hard work practising your bad habits or your old beliefs. If you think about the amount of time you spend practising *not* changing, it's no surprise that with little actual effort you become an expert at it! Change does require a certain amount of maintenance, and constant alterations may be needed, but just as a rudder on a sailing boat guides it from one place to another, conscious effort can guide your change and keep you on course to achieving what you want. The conscious effort you apply will in turn become your habit breaker, with each effort eventually becoming a subconscious action.

 **Task**

Section your life into parts that can be easily recognized; a storage system for your mind where you can place all of the bits needed for you to achieve a life full of success and happiness. For example, the parts could be related to career, finances, health, or relationships.

- Take one section at a time and work out *exactly* what it is you want to change. You'll need to be specific down to the smallest detail – if in doubt, get it out!
- Get into your *true state*, your success state where there is no failure, only feedback from which to learn.
- Change the sub-modalities one at a time. So, what does it **look** like when you have successfully made the change; what does it **sound, smell, taste,** and **feel** like?
- Take massive action to make it your physical reality – adopt an attitude of *already having.*
- Experience the rewards and move forwards towards reaping the rewards.

## *Saving for a rainy day . . .?*

It has become customary within Western culture to follow the accepted pattern of education, employment, and retirement as outlined earlier. However, there is an add-on element in the pattern, and that is the **Will**. It seems an accepted cultural mind-set that we should save for retirement . . . then save for a rainy day when in retirement . . . then make sure not to spend too much so that we have something to leave behind for our children . . .

**I've chosen a different mind-set: don't save for a rainy day, invest for a brighter future.**

This mind-set has taken me a few years to develop but it works wonders in terms of creating a carefree and trusting future. The more you begin to trust your own mind; the more you trust that you're doing the right thing for *you*, the more de-cluttered your conscious thinking becomes as a consequence.

**Achieving a clear mind is the highest form of achievement.**

The fun starts here! What are you going to do with all the newly acquired free space in your mind? This is a powerfully motivational element of change . . . see yourself in a future with you doing exactly as you wish, then change "I wish" for "I will"!

I love the idea of a "bucket list". A bucket list is essentially a "things to do before you die" list, or put another way, a list of things to do before you "kick the bucket"! In the 2007 film *The Bucket List*, Morgan Freeman and Jack Nicholson star as two terminally ill men who set about completing their own bucket lists before they die. Their "road trip" takes them around the world and sees them taking part in everything from skydiving to riding a motorbike on the Great Wall of China. However, for me, the most touching part of the story is the inclusion of "wishes" that money can't buy on the list. These include "laugh till I cry" and "help a complete stranger for the good" – both of which are crossed off the list during the course of the film. The idea of kicking the bucket and taking a sense of completion with you is an amazing concept, and one that we should all aspire to . . . regardless of current health, age, status, or anything else. **Do something NOW that will change your life and your lasting legacy. Do the impossible with your new positive mind-set.**

**Do not accept "impossible" . . . accept "I-am-possible" instead.**

Make your life a fantastic reflection of what is perfect for *you*, but don't aim for *perfection*, work towards doing your best in everything you do and pushing the boundaries of what it's possible for you to achieve in life by choosing to step out of your comfort zone.

 **Task**

Three stages to immediate wellbeing and improvement . . . do it right now!

**One:**

**On a scale of 1–10, where are you now (currently) in terms of the following:**

**Lifestyle** – this includes career, relationships, friendship and family, wealth, etc. . . . and all other aspects that you have included in your personal description.

**Health** – this is commonsense, but it is important to understand how your current physical health compares with what it should be. Overall health also includes mental health, but make physical health your primary concern and arrange to have a medical "check-up" with your doctor or health professional if needed.

A check-up will provide you with answers to health concerns such as high or low blood pressure, weight – including your body fat percentage – and any other issues relevant to your age and gender. Being honest about your health and gathering hard facts is a big step towards being able to make essential changes happen. But remember, this is a complete overhaul of your lifestyle that must be legacy driven, *not* target driven.

**Fitness** – this area will greatly depend on your overall health, and your definition of fitness may also be dependent on your current interests and activities. For this reason, score your current level of fitness in terms of "fitness for purpose"! Are you fit enough to do the things you want to do to the level you want to be able to do them? For example, you might be fit enough to walk around the shops but you might want to be fit enough to walk up Kilimanjaro.

*(Continued)*

Two:

On the same 1–10 scale, where do you *want to be* in each of the above?

Three:

Move forward 100 years and ask yourself . . .

- What will history say about you in relation to all of the above?
- How will you be remembered by your ancestors?

Avoid making mountains out of molehills by making something more than it is, but don't settle for things being as they are either; make things what you want them to be. If you can make everything you do in your life reflect on your life in a positive way then you are setting the stones of your lasting legacy of a life lived with an inner smile.

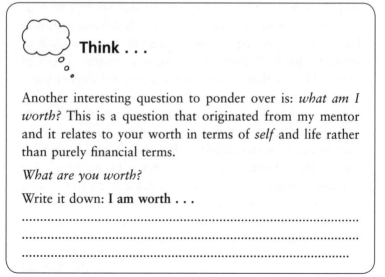

**Think . . .**

Another interesting question to ponder over is: *what am I worth?* This is a question that originated from my mentor and it relates to your worth in terms of *self* and life rather than purely financial terms.

*What are you worth?*

Write it down: **I am worth** . . .

..............................................................................

..............................................................................

..............................................................................

We all seek significance in life, whether it's via acceptance in society or by doing something unusual and different that makes us stand out! You have the freedom to do as you please with your life. You can choose to book an around the world trip; you can choose to live an alternative lifestyle and go off grid; and you can choose to quit the job you hate and become self-employed. These are all choices that are yours to make, no one else can make them for you, so why do we rarely make these radical changes? Well, some people do: some people will leave the UK with nothing more than a tooth-brush and a passport and head off to Africa for a month, others of course will remain slightly more cautious and will take steps to gain a little more security before taking this kind of massive action . . . but then still do it. The point I'm getting at is there are no "unrealistic goals" to set yourself in life. I'm not a fan of target driven goals, but in terms of setting yourself a legacy driven goal there are no limits. Your life, your legacy . . . the way you live your life and the way you are remembered is ultimately *your* choice.

*"If you can dream it, you can achieve it"*
Walt Disney

As mentioned earlier, I would love to have a time machine in which to go back and watch the many geniuses of our time at work. I'd love to know what strategies they used to cope with "failure" and I'd really love to know what thought processes inspired them to take action on what others often saw as radical new projects. One person I would particularly like to have met is Walt Disney. Disneyland is his lasting legacy . . .

> To all who come to this happy place; welcome. Disneyland is your land. Here age relives fond memories of the past . . . and here youth may savour the challenge and promise of the future. Disneyland is dedicated to the ideals, the dreams and the hard facts that have created America . . . with the hope that it will be a source of joy and inspiration to all the world.

## Passing on

The majority of people who knew of Walt Disney's "Disney-land" plans thought he was mad! Disney himself, of course, had the strength of character to *believe* in his dream and took action to turn that dream into a reality, despite being surrounded by doubters.

Disney had a vision and he *knew* that his vision would become a reality. Sadly, Disney died before the gates of Disneyland opened to the public, but his death did not end his dream . . . it lives on in his lasting legacy. Look back at your vision board, or take action to create one now if you have not already done so. At home, we have a family board as well as our own individual boards. It's fair to say that these boards rarely get much conscious attention, but the simple act of adding an inspiring image or removing an item that's no longer relevant from time to time is enough to allow your subconscious to make a note. Just as you may fail to notice all of the tiny cracks on a pavement you regularly walk along, your subconscious will note them every time.

 **Task**

Make a vision board a yearly ritual, perhaps even a family event, and get the kids involved by asking them to add their own meaning to each of the following:

- **Fun & Recreation** (re-creation) – add items or images that represent your "dreams" in terms of living a fun-filled life
- **Personal Growth** (aimed at a fulfilled outcome)
- **Relationship** (relation-ship; the vessels of communication)
- **Health** (both physical and mental)
- **Family & Friends**
- **Physical Environment**
- **Finances**

Remember, *perfection is achieved not when there is nothing more to add, but when there is nothing left to take away.* Your vision board should always be a representation of your "perfect" life with nothing left to take away. However, this should not prevent you from adding new things. Keep your life exciting by varying your interests. Add new things that fire your imagination and motivate you to "give it a go" – they can always be removed again if the spark proves to be short lived!

## Tell everyone or keep it to yourself?

Should you tell everyone about your plans and the lasting legacy you want to leave, or should you keep yourself to yourself? There are two trains of thought on this: the first is to keep it to yourself, then if you fail only you will know; and the second is to tell everyone so that you will have a sense of accountability over whether you actually take action to achieve what you want to achieve.

In my world it's neither one; I keep it neutral. If someone asks, why not tell them? If no one asks, there's no need to go out of your way to say anything. My reasons for this approach are simple. The only people who will be interested in knowing about your plans and the changes you are making are those closest to you, and they will already sense the changes. Your journey will not re-inform them or change how they see you, only your success will. Anyone else outside of your personal circle will generally only pay attention once they start to see the changes you are making and the benefits you are realizing through your change . . . *then* they'll be interested!

However, **be a reader then a leader**. You already know of the benefits of sharing your ideas and the importance of *reading* in order to then *lead*. Share your ideas with anyone who will listen, and the more who listen the more change will happen. I have always shared everything I learn, not because I wish to brag, but because I truly believe that the more people have a better overall understanding of all things, the more they will endeavour to have a better understanding of life and, as a result, this will better our ability to understand and communicate with one another.

Not everyone I meet holds the same view, and I am often surprised by the number of people I come across on my travels who claim ownership over information they have, making them reluctant to share it with others around them or reciprocate in any way with those who provided it. It has always struck me as being slightly odd that certain individuals will wait until an event has come to a standstill or things go wrong before saying, "Oh, I saw that coming all along" or "I could have told you that would happen."

Of course, not everyone will listen! Those who don't want to listen to your ideas are those who are unlikely to change or to follow the same path as you anyway. However, those who do are likely to spread your ideas and concepts and, just as importantly, your passion. These are the people who will support the infrastructure of the temple you are building; they add strength to your foundations, allowing you to continue building a lasting legacy.

## Don't be a puppet on a string . . .

It's very easy in this modern age to accept everything we are being told via the many media outlets to be the truth. Take car manufacturers for example; with their advertising campaigns, they can convince us that a certain type of car makes us really "cool"; really "distinguished"; really "sexy"; a real "family man"; a real "independent woman; or virtually "indestructible" on the road. You name it, there's a car that can do it for you! Any advertising campaign that "promises" some form of desirable change . . . *this product will make you younger; slimmer; more muscular; or irresistible to the opposite sex* . . . can be surprisingly effective in terms of boosting sales, and it would seem there's no limit to the marketing extremes some companies will go to in an effort to get you spending.

The best purchase for you is the purchase you need to make, not the purchase you are *told* you need to make. The same can be applied to your beliefs: when you think about the number of things we are told to believe in society, there is rarely a chance for any of us to make our own choices. Our main "puppeteers" are unfortunately usually those closest to us. Very often without any conscious thought, they pass on their beliefs . . . they *design* our thoughts and our behaviours by passing on what they believe to be the truth.

Nurture your mind with new learning and find your own truth. Learning new skills and trying new things is known to keep our minds alert into old age – but contrary to popular advertising, you don't need to buy a "brain trainer" to exercise your mind! Getting involved in something new not only increases your learning and broadens your horizons, sharing a new interest with another person can also bring about some exciting diversions in your thinking patterns.

## But life is all about balance . . .

Lifelong learning is definitely a part of my alternative view of life, but so is lifelong employment and lifelong retirement.

It's all about balance. We use expressions such as, "*Chasing* dreams" or "*Working* towards a goal" to describe our desire to keep moving and keep improving in life, but life should not be all work and no play . . . we need to learn how to relax. I know, learning how to relax doesn't sound like something you would associate with taking massive action – quite the opposite! But, taking time out of your busy schedule to relax and unwind is essential to your overall health and, without adequate rest, your body is unable to recover and repair itself after the stresses of everyday life. Personally, I attempt to sleep for about 10 hours a day and although some see it as wasting my time – with comments along the lines of "You have plenty of time to sleep when you're dead" – my response is always to point out that an engine performs better when filled with fuel!

## Get some quality "zeds"!

Sleep, and our need for it, has been the subject of countless scientific studies for many years, but we still don't have any concrete answers to the question of why we sleep. We know a lot about sleep – we understand sleep patterns, for example – and we know about the many detrimental physical effects a lack of sleep has on an individual, but we don't really have an understanding of exactly how much sleep is the "right" amount or why there's such a wide variation in the amount of sleep each of us finds ideal to function at our best.

For most us, one third of our lives will be spent asleep! That does sound like a huge chunk of life to devote to being blissfully unaware of the world, so why do we need so much sleep?

The main reasons put forward by scientific research include:

- **Recuperation** – sleep allows your body to recuperate from the activities of the day.
- **Maintenance** – sleep is essential to the maintenance of cognitive skills; meaning to be able to speak normally, think efficiently, and remember everything that's going on, we need to sleep. Inadequate sleep impairs all of the above and we know that there's a connection between sleep and brain development (which is why babies need sleep and why adolescents appear to take up residence in their beds!).

Of course, for most of us, a lack of sleep leads to general grumpiness and an inability to think about anything other than when it's time to go to bed! Sleep deprivation experiments (under controlled circumstances) have shown that staying awake for 17 hours has the same effect on your ability to concentrate as drinking two glasses of wine. Interestingly, two glasses of wine (or a 0.05 per cent alcohol level in your blood) is the legal limit in the UK for drinking and driving! Clearly, a lack of sleep can have serious consequences for drivers and, in many major incidents that involve "operator error," a lack of sleep is often found to be the cause.

Inadequate sleep effectively slows your physical responses but, as any new parent will tell you, sleep deprivation also impacts your emotional health. A lack of quality sleep can undoubtedly affect an individual's ability to cope with issues or happenings that might otherwise be taken in their stride. Tiredness often leads to emotional outbursts and "out of character" behaviours, and if anyone is going to make a mountain out of a molehill, it's going to be someone who is over-tired and in need of some quality rest and relaxation.

**In order to take massive action, take time out for rest and relaxation.**

*"A good laugh and a long sleep are the best cures in the doctor's book"*

Irish proverb

## *Your mind needs structure . . .*

Just as a builder can start to build from structured, detailed plans, you can begin to build your temple by giving your mind a structured plan or map. Babies and young children need a clear routine, soldiers and servicemen need a clear routine, and your mind needs a clear routine. Our minds need clarity . . . clarity in our thoughts allows for clarity in our actions.

Think about it for a moment; do you work better when you have drawn out each day in your diary into hour by hour slots? Do you work best by knowing where it is you need to be at any given time, and thereby ensuring that you always have plenty of time in between each task to arrive on time at the next? Or do you function better when things are left to chance and you make decisions on the hop? I am fairly sure that almost everyone works best with detailed structure in their daily lives. The reason for this is simple; the mind likes to know what, when, why, who, and where. When you know these things, you have clarity, and with clarity your day runs smoother and every task completed becomes much more enjoyable.

> **See to it that everything you do in the course of your everyday life demonstrates importance and significance. Give your mind the clarity it needs to demonstrate the true you and the best you in everything you do.**

Taking caring of ourselves and giving ourselves every opportunity to enjoy life to the full should be part of everyone's legacy. There's a saying "It's not just about adding years to your life, it's about adding life to your years" and these are wise words. When you have life in your years, you have all the energy you need to build your lasting legacy. Our energy has to go somewhere, and this is something I gained a clearer understanding of when mourning the loss of a loved one. I always had a sense of feeling her presence; I could feel the energy of her presence and I am sure the energy I could feel was the very same energy she used when she was alive. Her energy brought about positive emotions when she was living and it has continued to bring the same positive emotions, even though the physical aspects of the relationship have now ended. The positive emotions can still be relived in just the same way, just by thinking of her.

> *"Everyone must leave something behind when he dies . . . Something your hand touched some way so your soul has somewhere to go when you die . . . It doesn't matter*

*what you do, so long as you change something from the way it was before you touched it into something that's like you after you take your hands away"*
Ray Bradbury, *Fahrenheit 451*, 1953

Moving on from negative emotions is not always easy but it's important to avoid thinking of relationships or situations coming to an *end*. Choose to think of these happenings or *redirections* in your journey or *alterations* to the structure of your temple as you continue to build your lasting legacy. Having an *end* is all too final and, as you know, I'm not a fan of finality. The end is terminal, and something we only achieve when we pass on to the next life.

There is never a dead-end on your journey in this life . . . they just didn't build the road any further. It's time to pick up your tools and get building!

## Leaving a legacy checklist

- ☐ Accept that it's not the end that's important, it's the path you take
- ☐ Choose to let go of excess baggage
- ☐ Accept that if you were not born with it, you *do not* have to accept it
- ☐ Choose not to accept the impossible
- ☐ Accept that change is only as difficult as *you* make it
- ☐ Choose to give your mind and your life structure

# PICK UP YOUR TOOLS

L et's begin by taking three simple steps to change:

1. Understand the difference between the Present, the Past, and the Future.
2. Disassociate yourself with the Past.
3. Appreciate the unpredictability of the Future.

## Improve your communication skills and you'll change your outlook

Listeners make the best communicators: fact! Over the coming days, whether at work, home, or just out in public, follow these simple alterations and you'll be surprised by just how much you missed before.

Work on the following:

- Use your internal voice to communicate with yourself in a positive manner; think about the words you use.

Do they communicate in the positive or in the negative? Adopt a positive communication plan and change any negative.

- Look at your surroundings; clear your mind of any thoughts and just listen. This task can seem strange to start with, but just as a hunter listens to their environment for potential food, your mind will feed on the learning we once only appreciated subconsciously.

- Focus on others; the more you focus on others the more you are able to learn about what really makes them tick. Is it the way that they smile? How do they use their voice, and how do they use their body movements to show how they feel?

- A step towards a better you; improve your posture. It is said that 55 per cent of our communication is delivered through our body language. Make a conscious effort to correct your posture, as even a slight alteration can bring about a totally different perspective on external and internal events.

- Set yourself a target of pausing in between listening and speaking; allow your mind to digest the thoughts and then communicate knowing the full picture rather than second-guessing the remaining interaction.

## Get into the present

A lot can be said about ensuring that your heart and your mind are on the same path. From my own experiences, if they are not, a lot tends to be missed or there's a lack of motivation to make it work. The reason for this is a question of values.

If there is a discrepancy between our deeper values and the process being acted out via our conscious thought, then there is a non-congruent sensory output that will affect our behaviour on a subconscious level. The key to successful change is to align both.

## Remember your legacy statement

One thing that has always interested me is whether change can make you happy. By this I mean: will change in the many areas of our life that we usually reflect upon when thinking about life *actually* make any difference to happiness? These areas are usually divided into career, relationships, health, etc.; however, the question being asked shouldn't be "Will this make me happy?" but "How is this going to make me happy?"

The reason for this is very simple; the small change in linguistics will make a huge change to the way you produce the results internally. To understand at a deeper level, you must agree that happiness is something you *can* achieve, that it's a strength you hold within you, and something you are able to work towards – effectively a goal.

**Knowing the meaning:**

Happiness means something different to each of us, and no two people will define it in the same way. This means that finding your own motivation is key to finding *your* understanding of happiness.

Ask yourself:

- What is the most amount of motivation you can deal with?
- What would you be feeling if you were to achieve motivation at its peak?
- How would it feel, and how would you know that you had achieved it?

These are the sorts of questions you should use to start your happiness wheel moving. The more you increase the speed of the wheel, the faster your change will come about.

## Make change happen

Deciding *what* you want to change is a great starting point, but the statement must then evolve into "*How* can I change?" If you can master the answer to this question in a way that's specific to you then you will be able to *make change happen*, no matter what the circumstances in terms of relationships, work, money . . . the list goes on. Identifying your strategies for change is your goal, *not* the by-product of change.

**What we believe is true is what will become the truth** . . . this has become an affirmation I use on a regular basis, especially when faced with a task that just seems to be a struggle. Another is "If someone else has done it then so can I," and these simple affirmations have carried me through many, many challenges, both physical and mental (including Tough Guy adventure races, marathons, and business matters).

Take moment to think about a change that has been delayed in your life, and ask yourself what *not* making the change has restricted you from doing. You might find it helpful to write a physical list, or perhaps just meditate on it for a while and visualize a turn of events where the change has already happened.

## Lasting change is the ultimate change

So what's the difference between change and lasting change? Do you see them as one and the same? In fact, they are very different. Change can happen and then revert back to the former situation; a relationship may dissolve only to reunite, for example, and the weather is constantly changing! Just as changes in the weather can generate positive or negative emotions – happiness on sunny days, sadness on rainy days – changes in your life can generate a similar effect.

Lasting change or permanent change is change that involves taking radical (massive) action to change the imprint of your life. These are directional changes that will positively scar your life and become a point you can reflect on and learn from for the rest of your life. Daytime TV is littered with people who have made radical changes; they may, for example, have complained about the British weather so much over the years that they upped sticks and moved to a climate that has allowed them to remove that "lifestyle complaint"!

In the process of making a lasting change, you'll meet more external resistance. I am always reminded of resistance when changing the tyre on my car! It's not the easiest of tasks, but without the resistance the wheel wouldn't stay in place and keep my family safe. When removing the wheel from the car, a degree of resistance is required in order for change to happen, but further resistance is required when making the change. Resistance is therefore a two-way process; it happens when attempting to make the change, but also when the change is happening.

This analogy can be applied to making change happen in your life, but unfortunately it's not often used the right way. The more change is seen by those who are not making changes in their own lives, the more they will tell you that there is *no need* for change.

Over the years, as my success has grown, the number of "true" friends I have has dwindled. This is not because I have changed as a person, but because their representation of me has changed. Although it preyed on my mind at first, after a small amount of reflection and going through the tools I use with clients, the answer became clear: others feel threatened when you appear to be moving and they appear to be standing still . . . stagnant.

**Choose not to stand still; choose to move forwards, one step at a time, on *your* journey towards building a temple and leaving a lasting legacy . . . *your* legacy.**

# ABOUT BENJAMIN BONETTI

Benjamin Bonetti is considered one of the leading authorities within the self-help arena and has produced several leading hypnosis products.

Bonetti promotes and writes about the power of positive thinking and the essential need to take massive action. He is known to talk about his early struggles and refers to them in several of his early written pieces as the building blocks to his success.

Over the last 10 years his therapy techniques and bullish tactics have attracted many critics who believe that the no-nonsense approach can be interpreted as too forceful, especially to those with more sensitive issues. Bonetti, however, believes that it is this technique that is often overlooked by more "fluffy" type therapies and is the reason behind relapses.

Bonetti started his career in the British Army, serving for several years until later pursuing his dream of owning his own business; his entrepreneurial spirit has led him to own several businesses and later establish Benjamin Bonetti Ltd.

Bonetti has several well-known family links, and is related to Peter Bonetti (The Cat) the English goal keeper whose successful career saw him playing for both Chelsea and England during the 1970s.

Outside of business, Bonetti has been seen to promote the "voice" of the youth and during 2004 stood for local election, as the youngest person in history for that Council. Bonetti is also a keen and active conservationist, and volunteers for various countryside management organizations.

Although many of Bonetti's clients still remain unknown, he is often spotted behind the scenes at events supporting known A-list celebrities and artists. During a 2009 New Year's Day interview with the BBC Asian Network, Bonetti was referred to as a "celebrity must have secret weapon."

The success of his personal development audio recordings have led to them being available internationally, including in the UK, Ireland, Mexico, the USA, Australia, New Zealand, and Hong Kong.

http://www.benjaminbonetti.com

@benbonetti

Facebook: Benjamin Bonetti

## Also available from Benjamin Bonetti

Books

- *Fat Body Fat Mind*: Createspace, 2012 – ISBN 1479167355
- *Don't Struggle Quietly*: Createspace, 2012 – ISBN 1475153422
- *Inspirational & Motivational Quotes*: Createspace, 2010 – ISBN 1456333658
- *Entrepreneurs Always Drive On Empty*: Createspace, 2010 – ISBN 1453771093

Seminars & Training:

- The Law Of Attraction – The Truth
- NLP Practitioner Training UK & Overseas
- NLP Master Practitioner Training UK & Overseas
- Fat Body, Fat Mind – Coming Soon

Bonetti has produced a wide range of Hypnosis CDs and MP3s. The value of these is unknown to date, but consist of one of the largest ranges of hypnosis recordings by any one person.

2013 Advance Hypnotic Technique Audio CDs

- The Easy Way to Lose Weight with Hypnosis, Audiogo: 2013. ISBN 1471326284
- The Easy Way to Beat Insomnia and Sleep Easy with Hypnosis, Audiogo: 2013. ISBN 1471326322
- The Easy Way to Increase Self Confidence with Hypnosis, Audiogo: 2013. ISBN 1471326306

- The Easy Way to Stop Smoking with Hypnosis, Audiogo: 2013. ISBN 1471326314
- The Easy Way to Become Stress Free with Hypnosis, Audiogo: 2013. ISBN 1471326292

## 2013 Advance Hypnotic Technique Audio MP3s

- The Easy Way to Lose Weight with Hypnosis, Audiogo: 2013. ASIN: B00ANZ392S
- The Easy Way to Increase Self-Confidence with Hypnosis, Audiogo: 2013. ASIN: B00ANZ32ZW
- The Easy Way to Stop Smoking with Hypnosis, Audiogo: 2013. ASIN: B00ANZ37DO
- The Easy Way to Beat Insomnia and Sleep Easy with Hypnosis, Audiogo: 2013. ASIN: B00ANZ38CY
- The Easy and Original Hypnotic Gastric Band, Audiogo: 2013. ASIN: B00ANZ36OY
- The Easy Way to Relax during Pregnancy, Audiogo: 2013. ASIN: B00ANZ30R2
- The Easy Way to Beat Nail Biting with Hypnosis, Audiogo: 2013. ASIN: B00ANZ31K8
- The Easy Way to Improve Self-Belief with Hypnosis, Audiogo: 2013. ASIN: B00ANZ326G
- The Easy Way to Overcome Anxiety with Hypnosis, Audiogo: 2013. ASIN: B00ANZ35EU
- The Easy Way to Become Stress Free with Hypnosis, Audiogo: 2013. ASIN: B00ANZ3036

# INDEX